Learning Style in Education

ABOUT THE AUTHOR

Dr. S. K. PANNEER SELVAM is born in Salem - Valappady of Tamil Nadu. He started his career as school teacher in New Delhi in the year 1991. He joins as lecturer in DIET, perundurai of Erode in 2000. Bharathiyar University were gave the Philosophy in Doctorates in Language and Education. He is the seventh diploma holder from National University of Educational Planning and Administration (NUEPA), New Delhi in 2002. In 2005, the Tamil Nadu government was given the 'Excellence Award' for his unrivalled teaching activities and some organization also. He has published more than hundreds of Research Papers and books in the field of Education. At present he is working in the department of Education, Bharathidasan University, Tamil Nadu.

Mr. BABU THOMAS obtained his Master of Education and Master of Arts in Malayalam from Mahatma Gandhi University, Kottayam. He earned his Master of Science in Counsellingand Family Therapy (M.Sc-CFT) from IGNOU, New Delhi and in Applied Psychology from Bharathiar University, Coimbatore. He got his Post Graduate Diploma in Child, Adolescent and Family Counselling (PGD-CAFC) from Kerala University and Diploma in Training and Development (D-TD) from Indian Society for Training and Development (ISTD), New Delhi. He is a holder of UGC - NET (Education), SET, K-TET, Account Test & KER. He has 27 years of teaching experience in various reputed schools. At present working as a teacher in St. Ephrem's Higher Secondary School, Mannanam, Kottayam, Kerala. He received Air India – MalayalaManorama BOLT Award, All India AwardeeTeacher's Gurusreshta Award, MalankaraOrthodox Syrian Church Acharya Award. He is a Research Scholar in Education in Bharathidasan University, Tiruchirappalli, Tamil Nadu.

ABOUT THE BOOK

Education is probably the single most important function of human civilization, not merely the formal education system but the broader question of educating human beings around the world. Recent breakthroughs in communication technology have given us immense possibilities in this regard. Teachers have to develop competence in teaching in the digital world order and redefine their role in technology based learning. The term "information explosion" really means an explosion of knowledge. In a world of science and technology it is education that determines the level of property, welfare and security of the people.

❐

Learning Style in Education

Dr.S.K.Panneer Selvam
Assistant Professor, Department of Education
Bharathidasan University, T.N.,India

Babu Thomas
St. Ephrem's Higher Secondary School
Mannanam, Kottayam
Kerala

AMIGA PRESS INC.

AMIGA PRESS INC.
H.O:- 28-A, Indra Park, St.No-9
Near-Chander Nagar, Krishna Nagar
Delhi: - 110051 (India)
Tel: - 011-22504028, +91-98736-57000
Email: - amigapress@gmail.com
info@amigapress.co.in
amigaeditorial@gmail.com
amigapub@gmail.com

Website: - www.amigapress.co.in

This edition is published by Amiga Press Inc.

ISBN: 978-93-84533-70-0

First Published 2020

Printed and bound in India by Replika Press Pvt. Ltd.

Contents

❒

1

Attitude of Teacher Educators towards Blended Learning: A Study

Blended learning or hybrid learning describes a learning environment that either combines teaching methods, delivery methods, media formats or a mixture of all these. It also refers to the integrated learning activities such as a mixture of online and face-to-face learning. In other words, Blended learning is a mixture of e-learning and traditional types of learning. It is mentioned as the integrated combination of traditional learning with web-based online approaches, the combination of media and tools deployed in an e-learning environment and the combination of a number of pedagogical approaches. Elaborated Blended learning as a set of learning strategies or dimensions that mixes various event-based activities,including traditional instructor-led training, synchronous online conferencing or training and asynchronous self-paced study. Among the benefits of blended learning reported by recent research were provide students with more control over learning. Blended Learning in School Education provides a vision and a roadmap for School students to understand the content in blending face-to-face and online learning for engaging and meaningful learning experiences as like play way method.

Education is probably the single most important function of human civilization, not merely the formal education system but the broader question of educating human beings around the world. Recent breakthroughs in communication technology have given us immense possibilities in this regard. According to Don Berg, education is a process of cognitive cartography, mapping our experiences and finding a variety of reliable routes to optimal states when we find ourselves in non-optimal states. Blended learning develops individuals learning skills, meets their requirements for using technology, affords flexibility and convenience, provides access to those with job, family, distance barriers and reduces the educational cost for the students by the teacher. Blended Learning in Teacher Education approach combines face to face classroom methods. A thoughtfully designed integration of live and online methods in the post digital materials and methods in the post digital materials have served in a supplementary role helping to support face to face instruction for students of all ages and levels of learning. The best aspects of online instruction students in advance interactive experiences.

Need and Importance of the Study

Blended learning enables the teachers and students to understand the subject matter vividly. Worldwide there has been a strong push to get educational technology into the hands of teachers and students – yet it remains a reality that most teachers across the world continue to struggle with their day to day challenges in classrooms and remain completely un-impacted by technology even today. The primary reason for this is that most technology integration initiatives developed for schools ignore to look at the specific pain areas and real life challenges that teachers experience in classrooms. There is much talk nowadays about the need for blended learning in day today life. The development of vision, character, and competence in our young people is necessary to allow our nation to continue its role of world leader into the 21st century.

Statement of the Problem

Problem of the study is stated as attitude of teacher educators towards blended learning.

Objectives of the Study

1. To find out the significant difference in attitude of teacher educators towards blended learning with respect to gender.
2. To find out the significant difference in attitude of teacher educators towards blended learning with respect to educational qualification.
3. To find out the significant difference in attitude of teacher educators towards blended learning with respect to teaching experience.
4. To find out the significant difference in attitude of teacher educators towards blended learning with respect to optional subject teaching.

5. To find out the significant difference in attitude of teacher educators towards blended learning with respect to guidance provides to students.

Hypotheses of the Study

1. There will be a significant mean score difference in attitude of teacher educators towards blended learning with respect to gender.
2. There will be a significant mean score difference in attitude of teacher educators towards blended learning with respect to educational qualification.
3. There will be a significant mean score difference in attitude of teacher educators towards blended learning with respect to teaching experience.
4. There will be a significant mean score difference in attitude of teacher educators towards blended learning with respect to optional subject teaching.
5. There will be a significant mean score difference in attitude of teacher educators towards blended learning with respect to guidance provides to students.

Methodology of the Present Study

Research methodology is the description, explanation and justification of various methods of conducting research. Research studies adopting different methods, however do not as a rule, differ significantly in their procedures, selection, formation and definition of the problem, survey of related information, collection, analysis and interpretation of new data and reporting of the work done are steps of procedure common to all type of method of research. Here, the investigator used survey method for the present investigation. It is the most commonly used descriptive method in educational research. It is concerned with the present and attempts to determine the status of the phenomena under investigation.

The various types of survey and different techniques used in survey have their respective significance and value. In survey, practical remedies to solve and resolve problems can be put forward and these remedies will normally be efficacious because they are the outcome of scientific study and analysis.

Research Tool

For the present study, the researcher developed an own questionnaire to find out the Attitude of Teacher Educators towards Blended Learning with 40 items. On the basis of expert's opinions 10 items were omitted. The final scale consists of 30 items on the basis of two factors such as Personal and Teaching-Learning.

Scoring Procedure

Strongly Agree – 4, Agree – 3, Disagree – 2, Strongly Disagree – 1

Higher the score indicates the higher the level of attitude towards blended learning.

Population and Sample of the Present Study

The population of the study was secondary teacher educators in the round of Salem district. The researcher has selected 240 teacher educators as sample by using random sampling technique. The details of the sample were presented in the following table

TABLE. 1.1: Break-up of SampleAdministration of the Tool

Variables	Sub Variables	No. of Sample
Gender	Male	103
	Female	137
Age	Below 30	96
	30 & Above	144
Locality	Urban	116
	Rural	124
Marital Status	Married	178
	Unmarried	62
Educational Qualitification	P.G.	132
	M. Phil & Ph. D.	108
Teaching Experience	Below 5 Years	97
	5 years & Above	143
Locality of Institution	Urban	83
	Rural	124
Optional Subject teaching	Science	144
	Language & Social Science	96
Guidance Provide to Students	Yes	43
	No	197

Administration of the Tool

The final tool was administered to 240 Teacher Educators from Salem district. Directions were given to the samples before administering the tool. And the subjects were requested to give their views and opinions in the proper places. They were assuring that the information given by them would keep confidential. After administering the tool, the responses were evaluated and scored on the basis of the scoring procedures.

Data Analysis

After the collection of pertinent data through the use of appropriate tools and techniques, the next step is the process of analysis and interpretation in the research. The collected data were analyzed by using appropriate statistical techniques that are Mean, SD- Standard Deviation and t- test.

Analysis and Interpretation

Hypotheses Testing

Hypothesis 1

There will be a significant mean score difference in attitude of teacher educators towards blended learning with respect to gender.

TABLE. 1.2: Mean Score Difference in Blended Learning among Teacher Educators with Respect to Gender

Factors	Variables	N	Mean	S.D.	t-Value	Level of Significance at 0.025 Level
Personal	Male	103	43.84	3.97	1.63	NS*
	Female	137	44.69	3.91		
Teaching-Learning	Male	103	57.91	5.3	0.78	NS
	Female	137	58.46	5.38		
Total	**Male**	**103**	**101.76**	**7.2**	**1.52**	**NS**
	Female	**137**	**103.15**	**6.8**		

• N.S – Denotes Not Significant.

According to the table 5.2, the calculated t- value is less than the table value at 0.05 level. So, there is no significant difference in attitude towards blended learning among teacher educators with respect to the gender. So the hypothesis No.1 is rejected. Further, the male and female teacher educators are does not differ in attitude towards blended learning.

Hypothesis 2

There will be a significant mean score difference in attitude of teacher educators towards blended learning with respect to educational qualification.

TABLE. 1.3: Mean Score Difference in Blended learning among Teacher Educators with Respect to Educational Qualification

Factors	Variables	N	Mean	S.D.	t-Value	Level of Significance at 0.025 Level
Personal	P.G.	132	44.36	3.81	1.55	NS
	M. Phil & Ph. D	108	45.11	3.56		
Teaching-Learning	P.G.	132	57.23	5.32	1.51	NS
	M. Phil & ph. D	108	58.23	4.87		
Total	**P.G.**	**132**	**101.59**	**7.22**	**1.96**	**NS**
	M. Phil & Ph. D	**108**	**103.34**	**6.4**		

According to the above table 5.6, the calculated t- value is less than the table value at 0.05 level. So, there is no significant difference in attitude of teacher educators towards blended learning with respect to educational qualification. So, the hypothesis No.5 is rejected. Further, the P.G and M. Phil and Ph.D holders are homogeneous in attitude towards blended learning.

Hypothesis 3

There will be a significant mean score difference in attitude of teacher educators towards blended learning with respect to teaching experience.

TABLE. 1.4: Mean Score Difference in Blended learning among Teacher educators with Respect to Teaching Experience

Factors	Variables	N	Mean	S.D.	t-Value	Level of Significance at 0.025 Level
Personal	Below 5 years	97	44.02	4.11	1.99	Significant
	5 years & Above	143	44.72	3.86		
Teaching-Learning	Below 5 years	97	57.2	5.15	2.61	Significant
	5 years & Above	143	58.97	5.18		
Total	**Below 5 years**	**97**	**101.22**	**7.75**	**2.14**	**Significant**
	5 Years & Above	**143**	**103.41**	**7.8**		

According to the above table 5.7, the calculated t- value is greater than the table value at 0.05 level. So, there is significant difference in attitude of teacher educators towards blended learning with respect to teaching experience. So the hypothesis No.6 is accepted. Further, the 5 years and above experienced teacher are superior in attitude towards blended learning.

Hypothesis 4

There will be a significant mean score difference in attitude of teacher educators towards blended learning with respect to optional subject teaching.

TABLE. 1.5: Mean Score Difference in Blended learning among Teacher Educators with Respect to Optional Subjects Teaching

Factors	Variables	N	Mean	S.D.	t-Value	Level of Significance at 0.025 Level
Personal	Science	144	44.57	3.79	1.54	NS
	Language & Social Science	96	43.8	3.77		
Teaching-Learning	Science	144	53.39	5.15	0.90	NS
	Language & Social Science	96	57.73	5.82		
Total	**Scinece**	**144**	**102.96**	**7.08**	**1.50**	**NS**
	Language & Social Science	**96**	**101.53**	**7.41**		

According to the above table 5.9, the calculated t- value is less than the table value at 0.05 level. So, there is no significant difference in attitude of teacher educators towards blended learning with respect to the Optional Subject teaching. So the hypothesis No.8 is rejected. Further, the science and language and social science teacher educators are homogeneous in attitude towards blended learning.

Hypothesis 5

There will be a significant mean score difference in attitude of teacher educators towards blended learning with respect to guidance provides to students.

TABLE. 1.6: Mean Score Difference in Blended learning among Teacher Educators with Respect to Guidance Provide to Students

Factors	Variables	N	Mean	S.D.	t-Value	Level of Significance at 0.025 Level
Personal	Yes	43	43.86	3.43	1.40	NS
	No	197	44.78	3.96		
Teaching-Learning	Yes	43	57.05	5.1	1.60	NS
	No	197	58.45	5.21		
Total	**Yes**	**43**	**100.91**	**7.3**	**1.82**	**NS**
	No	**197**	**103.22**	**7.58**		

According to the above table 5.10, the calculated t- value is less than the table value at 0.05 level. So, there is no significant difference in attitude of teacher educators towards blended learning with respect to guidance provide to students. So, the hypothesis No.9 is rejected. Further, the selected independent variable does not influence in this study.

Findings of the Study

1. From the table 5.3, the calculated t- value is less than the table value at 0.05 level. So, there is no significant difference in attitude of teacher educators towards blended learning with respect to age. So the hypothesis No.2 is rejected. It is also reveals that the age factor does not influence the attitude towards blended learning.
2. According to the above table 5.6, the calculated t- value is less than the table value at 0.05 level. So, there is no significant difference in attitude of teacher educators towards blended learning with respect to educational qualification. So, the hypothesis No.5 is rejected. Further, the P.G and M. Phil and Ph.D holders are homogeneous in attitude towards blended learning.
3. According to the above table 5.7, the calculated t- value is greater than the table value at 0.05 level. So, there is significant difference in attitude of teacher educators towards blended learning with respect to teaching experience. So the hypothesis No.6 is accepted. Further, the 5 years and above experienced teacher are superior in attitude towards blended learning.
4. According to the above table 5.9, the calculated t- value is less than the table value at 0.05 level. So, there is no significant difference in attitude of teacher educators towards blended learning with respect to the Optional Subject teaching. So the hypothesis No.8 is rejected. Further, the science and language and social science teacher educators are homogeneous in attitude towards blended learning.
5. According to the above table 5.10, the calculated t- value is less than the table value at 0.05 level. So, there is no significant difference in attitude of teacher educators towards blended learning with respect to guidance provide to students. So, the hypothesis No.9 is rejected. Further, the selected independent variable does not influence in this study.

Educational Implications

1. This study will help to develop positive attitude towards blended learning among teacher educators.
2. This study will help to implement virtual learning concept.
3. This study will helpful to the future researchers in developing a new

research in understanding a difficult concept in a simpler way through the blended learning.

4. This research work will help to know the importance of blended learning and its practical knowledge in all levels of education.
5. Suggestions for Further Research
6. This kind of study may take up by other researchers by taking large number of samples and variables.
7. Similar study may take up by future researchers on analysis of attitude of teacher trainees towards blended learning.
8. This study may undertaken by future research scholars in the attitude of college teachers towards Blended learning.
9. Future researchers may take up a comparative study on conventional learning and Blended learning.

Conclusion

In this study, the researcher studied the attitude of teacher educators towards blended learning. The findings reveal that the teacher educators are better in attitude towards blended learning. The urban located teachers are superior than the rural teachers. Further, 5 and above 5 years experienced teachers are greater in attitude towards blended learning. Other selected variables are does not influence in this study.

❐

2

Awareness of Online Learning among Post Graduate Students: A Study

In order to capitalize on the potential of new technology, particularly digital technology as a learning tool, there is an urgent need of the professional development of teachers. It allows teachers to construct professional knowledge about pedagogy, content and technology as well as strategies for managing the changing classroom environments. Teachers have to develop competence in teaching in the digital world order and redefine their role in technology based learning. The term "information explosion" really means an explosion of knowledge. New frontiers of knowledge are opening day-by-day and the horizon of human knowledge and understanding is expanding very fast. In the present days all above mentioned knowledge information and skill is imparted by the education institutions. Online education originally began through various companies and their training courses. When a new employee was hired online training courses were used to prepare the employee.

New developments in the learning sciences and technologies provide opportunities to create well-designed, learner-centered, engaging, interactive, affordable, efficient, easily accessible, flexible, and meaningful, distributed and facilitated online-learning environment. New learning techniques have entered in the field of education. Every teacher at present should be required to function in such an environment. A teacher is no longer viewed as the transmitter of knowledge or dimensions of wisdom, but as a diagnostician, guide, assistant, whenever appropriate exchanger, stimulator, promoter and an interactive participant in the education process. Teachers have to develop competence in teaching in the digital world order and redefine their role in technology based learning.

Online Learning: Meaning

"Online learning is the process of education i.e., learning, teaching obtaining knowledge and skill through internet". The internet is method of communication, interaction, entertainment, health, trade and commerce, students can visit websites not only to download desired information but also to ask questions till out examination forms solving questions papers and learning information from the teacher so through online education student can learn acquire knowledge information and skill of particular work or job without attending any class but sitting in the house where internet is available.

How Online Education Works?

After researching the best accredited institution are required to apply to one of the college's degree programs. Once accepted into an online program students are asked to sign up for appropriate courses. After the registration process is complete and students are accepted into the program, the real work begins. Students begin their course studies by logging onto the internet. Once they're in their appropriate classroom they'll learn by reading assignments asking questions and receiving instructor feedback. Some courses even offer forums and chat rooms where students can gather with or without the instructor to discuss assignments. Finally students are graded on homework assignments final project and test scores.

Online Learning and Its Tools

There are many tools of communication on internet. They include E-mail listers, news group, internet conferencing etc,

1. **E-mail:** The desire to communicate is the essence of networking. E-mail is the most basic form of communication on the internet and by far the most popular one used in education and research. It facilitates communication form one person to another in the form of non-interactive transmission of text data graphics etc. it is very fast confidential and instills a sense of connectedness. Document can also be attached to e-mail messages.
2. **Listers:** Listers are also called mailing lists. They provide an opportunity for those in education and research to share ideas on common interests. These are usually used for discussions.

3. **Internet Conferencing:** It has great potential for learning in higher education. It facilitates greater opportunity for a dialogue between learners and the instructors as well as amongst the learners. These programmes require that both the users be connected to the internet simultaneously.
4. **E-Publishing:** Most of the publishers are choosing web as an access-medium using HTML to mark up the journal contents so that it can be read using a web browser. Most of the reputed publishers learned and commercial societies are hosting their products on the net.
5. **Library Services through the Internet:** Use of library and the use of internet are positively related to education attainment. Traditional information research tools and sources found in the libraries have been n recently supplemented by the information available on the internet. Digital library concept may be elaborated as a process of electronically acquiring, storing and disseminating the date to the users.
6. **E-learning:** E-learning is also called online learning. It refers to learning and other supportive resources that are available through a computer. In an online lesson, the computer display material in response to a learner's request. Here online systems refers to continuous and active interaction between two servers through the internet, E-learning is developed to apply information technology skills to education.

Need for the Study

The present study attempts to assess the online learning awareness among the Post Graduate students of Arts and Science colleges in Erode district. It also suggests methods to create sustain and improve the Post Graduate Students awareness of online learning.

Statement of the Problem

Being future professionals, Post Graduate students should be made aware of the importance of online-learning in the teaching learning process. In this backdrop, the present study attempts to find out the "awareness of online learning among Post Graduate students of Arts and Science Colleges in Erode District". It also suggests methods to improve and sustain the Post Graduate student's awareness of online learning.

Objectives of the Study

The objectives of the study are as follows:

1. To study the awareness of online learning among Post Graduate students of Arts and Science colleges in Erode district.

2. To find out whether there is any significant difference in the online learning awareness mean scores between male and female Post Graduate students.
3. To find out whether there is any significant difference between the mean scores of Post Graduate first year and second year students awareness on online learning.
4. To find out whether there is any significant difference between the mean scores of Post Graduate students of science and arts with regard to online learning awareness.

Hypotheses of the Study

In the light of the objectives, the following null hypotheses are formulated for testing.

1. Awareness on online learning among post graduate students of Arts and Science colleges in Erode district is not adequate.
2. There is no significant difference between mean score of awareness on online learning of Post Graduate male and female students.
3. There is no significantly difference between mean scores of awareness on online learning of Post Graduate first year and second year students.
4. There is no significant difference between mean scores of awareness on online learning of the Post Graduate students of science and arts.
5. There is no significant difference in the awareness mean scores of online learning between the Post Graduate students with computer knowledge and without computer knowledge.

Methodology in Brief

As the present study is descriptive by nature, normative survey method was adopted. As many as 250 Post Graduate students from various departments of Arts and Science colleges in Erode district were chosen as sample by using a simple random sampling technique.

Limitations of the Study

Though online-learning is a vast subject the investigator restricted himself only to limited area for this study. The investigation is only on awareness of online-learning among Post Graduate students of Arts and Science colleges in Erode district. The investigator has attempted to collect data from only six departments from Three Arts and science colleges in Erode district due to constrains of time and money.

Methods and Procedure

The investigator used a standardized from of questionnaire and the items were verified with the help of research guide and the subject experts. The tool was administered to the sample selected in Arts and science colleges in Erode District, data were collected from Post graduate students of various Departments.

Research Method

The investigator used normative survey method in this study to collect data from the Post Graduate students of Arts and Science colleges in Erode district. In this study the investigator used a questionnaire to collect the data from the respondents.

Construction of Research Tool

The investigator developed and used an online learning awareness questionnaire in order to find out the Post Graduate students' awareness about the online learning. As a first step, 40 items were given under various dimensions, in the form of an online learning awareness scale. The expert opinions were taken into account and on the basis of their remarks, some items were modified and some rewarded. Thus a total 30 statements were given up in the Questionnaire.

Description of Research Tool and Scoring

The research tool consisted of two parts, the part-A deals with General Information about the respondent and the part - B deals with Awareness on online learning questionnaire. The former part of the research tool was designed to seek information about the personal characteristics of the respondents such as sex, discipline; year of study, computer knowledge, place of stay etc., the later part of this tool was developed in order to study the Post Graduate students' awareness on online learning.

Validity of the Tool

Only highly discriminating items are included in the questionnaire. The content validity has been established by considering the experts view in the field of Educational Technology and Computer applications.

Pilot Study

The researcher conducted a pilot study to select and modify the tool. The researcher distributed and collected the tool from 50 Post Graduate students, who were studying various PG courses in Erode district.

Selection of the Sample

Random sampling technique was adopted for the present study. The sample of Post Graduate students was selected in a random manner. The sample selected from various Departments of Post Graduate students of Arts and Science colleges in Erode district were selected by using simple random sampling technique. Thus total of 250 students. The break-up of the sample was presented in table 2.1.

TABLE. 2.1: Break-up of the Final Sample

S.No.	Variables	Sub-variables	Sample	Total
1	Gender	Male	170	**250**
		Female	80	
2	Year of study	I year	119	**250**
		II year	131	
3	Discipline	Science	157	**250**
		Arts	93	
4	Computer knowledge	Knowing computer	223	**250**
		Not knowing computer	27	
5	Place of stay	Hosteller	47	**250**
		Day scholar	203	
6	Usage of internet	Department	129	**250**
		Browsing centre	92	
		Home	29	

Statistical Techniques Used

Statistical techniques serve the fundamental purpose of the descriptive and inferential analysis.

1. Mean and Standard Deviation
2. 't' test for determining the significance of difference between means of two sub-groups used in the study.

Analysis and Interpretation of Data

It is worthwhile to prepare a plan of analysis before the actual collection of data. Good, bar and scats suggests the four helpful modes to get start an analyzing the gathered data.

1. To think in terms of significant tables that the date permit.
2. To examine carefully the statement of the problem and earlier analysis and to study the original records of the data.
3. To get away from the date and to think about the problem in layman's terms or to actually discuss that problem with others.
4. To attack the data to make the various statistical calculations.

Data Analysis

Hypothesis: 1.

Awareness on Online learning among post graduate students of Arts and Science colleges in Erode district is not adequate

The hypothesis was tested using the mean scores of awareness on online learning among post graduate students of Arts and Science colleges in Erode district.

TABLE. 2.2: Mean and Standard Deviation for Awareness Score for the Total Students

S.No	Variable	N	Maximum	Mean	Standard Deviation
1	Awareness score	250	150	98.85	11.07

The mean and standard deviation for the total awareness score for the post graduate students are presented in the above table. The maximum possible score is 150, the mean value is found to be 98.85 i.e., more than 60 percent. Hence, the post graduate students in Erode district have above average level of awareness on online learning.

Hypothesis: 2.

There is no significant difference between mean scores of awareness on online learning of post graduate male and female students

The hypothesis was tested using 't' test. The 't; was computed to find out the significance of difference between the mean scores of awareness on online learning of post graduate male and female students.

TABLE. 2.3: Analysis of Sample in Terms of Gender

Variable	Sub variables	N	M	S.D	t-value	Significance at 0.05 level
Gender	Male	170	98.51	9.93	0.56	Not significant
	Female	80	99.45	13.23		

Critical value of 0.05 level = 1.98

Calculated 't' value = 0.56

The calculated 't' value 0.56 is less than the table value 1.98 corresponding to the 0.05 level of significance. This implies that the different in online learning awareness means scores under consideration is not significant. Hence, the null hypothesis is accepted. Therefore, it is concluded that the male and female post graduate students do not differ significantly regarding awareness on online learning. Further it reveals that, both male and female post graduate students have similar in their level of awareness on online learning.

Hypothesis: 3.

There is no significant difference between mean scores of awareness on online learning of post graduate first year and second year students

The hypothesis was tested using 't' test. The 't' was computed to find out the significance of difference between the mean scores of awareness on online learning among first year and second year students.

TABLE. 2.4: Analysis of Sample in Terms of Year of Study

Variable	Sub variables	N	M	S.D	t-value	Significance at 0.05 level
Year of study	I year	119	98.36	10.11	0.59	Not significant
	II year	131	99.19	11.92		

Critical value of 0.05 level = 1.98

Calculated 't' value = 0.59

The calculated 't' value 0.59 is less than the table value 1.98 corresponding to the 0,05 level of significance. This implies that the difference in awareness means scores under consideration is not significant. Hence, the null hypothesis is accepted.

Hypothesis: 4.

There is no significant difference between mean scores of awareness on online learning among the post graduate students of science and arts

The hypothesis was tested using 't' test. The 't' was computer to find out the significance of difference between the mean scores of awareness on online learning among the post graduate students of science and arts.

TABLE. 2.5: Analysis of Sample in Terms of Discipline

Variable	Sub variables	N	M	S.D	t-value	Significance at 0.01 level
Discipline	Science	157	100.54	12.06	5.12**	Significant
	Arts	93	95.98	8.63		

Critical value of 0.01 level =2.59

Calculated 't' value = 5.12

The calculated 't' value 5.12 is higher than the table value 2.59 corresponding to the 0.01 level of significance. This implies that the difference in the awareness means scores under consideration is statistically significant. Hence, the null hypothesis is rejected.

Hypothesis: 5.

There is no significant difference in the awareness means scores between the post graduate students with computer knowledge and without computer knowledge

The hypothesis was tested using 't' test the 't' was computer to find out the significance of difference between the mean scores of awareness of online learning if the post graduate students with and without computer knowledge.

TABLE. 2.6: Analysis of Sample in Terms of Computer Knowledge

Variable	Sub variables	N	M	S.D	t-value	Significance at 0.01 level
Computer Knowledge	Knowing computer	223	98.37	12.92	6.8**	Significant
	Not knowing computer	27	89.55	4.96		

Critical value of 0.01 level = 2.59

Calculated 't' value = 6.8

The calculated 't' value 6.8 is higher than the table value 2.59 corresponding to the 0.01 level of significance this implies that the difference in the awareness means scores under consideration is statistically significant. Hence, the null hypothesis is rejected.

Hypothesis: 6.

There is no significant difference in the awareness means score between hostellers and day scholars regarding online learning

The hypothesis was tested using 't' test. The 't' was computer to find out the significance of difference between the mean scores of awareness on online learning between the post graduate students of hosteller and day scholars.

TABLE. 2.7: Analysis of Sample in Terms of Place of Stay

Variable	Sub variables	N	M	S.D	t-value	Significance at 0.05 level
Place of stay	Hosteller	47	103.68	18.77	2.39*	Significant
	Day scholar	203	96.93	9.74		

Critical value of 0.05 level =1.98 Calculated 't' value =2.39

The calculated 't' value 2.39 is higher than the table value 1.98 corresponding to the 0.05 level of significance. This implies that the difference in the awareness means scores under consideration is statistically significant. Hence, the null hypothesis is rejected.

Hypothesis: 7.

There is no significant different in the awareness mean scores between the post graduate students who utilized internet at home browsing centre and at the department

The hypothesis was tested using 't' test. The 't' was computed to find out the significance of difference in awareness means scores between the students who utilized internet at home, browsing center and at the department.

TABLE. 2.8: Analysis of Sample in Terms of Usage of Internet

Variable	Sub variables	N	M	S.D	t – value	Significance at 0.05 level
Usage of Internet	Department	129	99.30	11.87	1.10	Not significant
	Browsing centre	92	97.67	9.55		
	Home	29	101.07	11.53	1.39	Not significant
	Browsing centre	92	97.67	9.55		
	Department	129	99.30	11.87	0.73	Not significant
	Home	29	101.07	11.53		

Critical value of 0.05 level = 1.98

Calculated 't' values = 1.10, 1.39 and 0.73

The calculated t values 1.10, 1.39, and 0.73 are less than the table value 1.98 corresponding to the 0.05 level of significance. This implies that the difference in the awareness mean scores under considerations is not significant. Hence, the null hypothesis is accepted.

Summary of Findings and Conclusion

A tool was developed and samples were selected, and then data were collected and analysed. Hypotheses were formulated and tested with the help of statistical techniques. Based on the data analysis and hypothesis testing a number of findings were found out.

The awareness of online learning is important among Post Graduate students / research scholars in order to implement the usage of it in a productive way in future. The present study attempts to assess the online learning awareness among the Post Graduate of Arts and Science colleges in Erode district. It also suggests methods to create sustain and improve the Post Graduate Students awareness of online learning.

Major Findings

1. It is concluded that the post graduate students of Arts and Science colleges in Erode district have considerable level of awareness on online learning as their awareness mean scores is found to be more than 60 percent.

2. It is concluded that the male and female post graduate students do not differ significantly regarding awareness on online learning. Further it reveals that, both male and female post graduate students have similar in their level of awareness on online learning.
3. It is concluded that the first year and second year students do not differ significantly, regarding awareness on online learning. Both first year and second year students have similar level of awareness with regard to online learning.
4. It is concluded that the post graduate students of science and arts differ significantly in respect of their awareness on online learning. Further the higher mean scores of the post graduate students of science have more aware of the online learning than the arts post graduate students.
5. It is concluded that the post graduate students differ significantly regarding awareness on online learning. Further the higher mean scores of the post graduate students with computer knowledge have more aware of than the post graduate students without computer knowledge in respect of their awareness on online learning.
6. It is concluded that the hosteller and day scholar student differ significantly regarding awareness of online learning. Further the higher mean sores of the post graduate students of hosteller have more aware of online learning than the day scholars.
7. It is concluded that the post graduate students who utilized internet at home, at browsing centre and at the department do not differ significantly with respect of their awareness on online learning.

Educational Implications

Based on the above given findings and conclusions, the present study offer the following suggestions and recommendations.

1. It is imperative that steps are taken to create comprehensive awareness of Online learning among the Post Graduate students of Arts and Science colleges in Erode district.
2. Steps must be taken to extent the scope of the ICT in Education cause of the Post Graduate Programme of Arts and Science colleges in Erode district.
3. Post Graduate Students are to be encouraged to visit the Online Learning portals and review them.
4. Steps must be taken to train the Post Graduate students of Arts and Science colleges in Erode district in access of online.

Suggestions for Further Research

Based on the findings and conclusion of the study, the investigator offers the following suggestions for further research:

1. As the present study has been taken up only with Post Graduate Students of Arts and Science colleges in Erode district as sample, studies with students of other universities as sample may be taken up for the further research.
2. Attempts may be taken to study Online Learning awareness among teachers of private, government and government aided schools teachers educators working in colleges of different types may also be taken as sample for further research.
3. This same study can be replicated with more advanced statistical analysis in terms of gender, locality, computer literacy, marital status, and other relevant variables.
4. Comparative studies can be taken up to compare the Online learning awareness of the scholars of this university with the scholars of other universities.

Conclusion

The above given review of related literature gave the investigator lots of insights in to the e-learning and guided the investigated in a systematic way. In this study, the investigator explain the method and procedure followed for the present study under the captions like selection of the tool, sampling techniques and collection of data. In this study various data collected from post graduate students of Arts and Science colleges in Erode district have been analysed and interpreted. Now with the increasing complexity of modern times, education faces ever-changing new demands, and mostly Post graduate students have to bear the brunt of the changes. Hence, the students need to be sensitive changes and the ready for changes. They have to possess awareness, knowledge and skills with regard to Online Learning.

❒

3

Awareness on Educational Television among the teacher Trainees: A Study

Educational Television (ETV) is a system that presents learning content in various subjects produced by an agency. It is a means of providing direct instruction (formal) as well as continuing education (non-formal). Educational inequality is a persistent problem in most countries, from both economic and socio-cultural viewpoints. ETV can promote the concept of equalization of educational opportunities by providing instructional actions that are so universal that they become specific to every viewer and are effective regardless of sex, race, ethnic background or economic condition. EDUSAT is the first exclusive satellite for serving the educational sector. It is specially configured to meet the growing demand for an interactive satellite based distance education system for the country through audio-visual medium, employing direct to home (DTH) quality broadcast. The ISRO scientists claim "the satellite will bring education to home (ETH) nearer". While scientists, economists, politicians and the common public talk so much about EDUSAT and its potentials, it is disheartening that it failed to create the much-needed sensation among the teaching community. In this aspect, this study is of great importance, as its findings will throw light on the Diploma level teacher trainees' ETV awareness, based on which decision with far-reaching implications can be taken to ensure effective utilization of the services in India. Besides, the study will give the necessary input for the planners and designers of pre-service training programmes and in-service training programme for the professional development of primary level teachers.

It has been a little over a decade since a television set became a part of the equipment of many Indian homes. And it became the part and parcel of our life within no time. When television began, there were great hopes and great fears concerning its possible effects. The optimists believed that it could educate children in the widest possible sense, giving them an opportunity to learn about science and human life in such a fascinating way that learning would be a joy instead of labour. And now, it's the time to think over the topic that whether this powerful medium is being utilized effectively in educational field or not.

Audio-Visual Aids

"Audio-visual aids are the different types of tools that appeal to the senses of learning and vision and are used in classrooms for presentation of abstract information". Today it has been proved beyond doubt by research and classroom experience that audio-visual aids can contribute effectively in learning.

Educational Television

Educational Television (ETV) is a system that presents learning content in various subjects produced by an agency. It is a means of providing direct instruction (formal) as well as continuing education (non-formal).

Types of Educational Television Programmes

ETV programmes are made available to the students in a variety of modes. Some of the most important types of ETV programmes are

- **Monologue:** A narrator narrates the aspects, interlacing it with visuals the illustrations.
- **Dialogue:** Conversation between two people.
- Interviews
- Panel Discussion
- Quiz
- Dramas
- Stimulated Classrooms
- Virtual Classrooms

Television as a means of Extending Children's Experience

TV in the classroom is truly what UNESCO has often called it "a window on the world". The programmes allow students to transcend the boundaries to space and time and to see society in new and diverse ways. The rural child sees life in the city and the urban child sees life in the country, various patterns of consumptions and economic structure, alternative religious forms, cultural patterns and sexual role models are made available on the television. ETV can promote the concept of equalization of educational opportunities by providing instructional actions that are so universal that they become specific to every viewer and are effective regardless of sex, race, ethnic background or economic condition.

ETV in India: A Historical Perspective

Television first came to India [named as Doordarshan (DD)] on September 15, 1959 as the National Television Network of India. The first telecast started on Sept. 15, 1959 in New Delhi.

Secondary School Television Project (1961)

This project was designed for the secondary school students of Delhi. With an aim to improve the standard of teaching in view of the shortage of laboratories, space, equipment and dearth of qualified teachers in Delhi, this project started on experimental basis in October 1961 for teaching Physics, Chemistry, English and Hindi for the students of Class XI.

Delhi Agriculture Television (DATV) Project-Krishi Darshan (1966)

This project, one of the largest techno-social experiments in human communication, was commissioned for the villagers and their Primary School children of selected 2330 villages in six states of India. It started on August 1, 1975 for a period of one year in six states namely Rajasthan, Karnataka, Orissa, Bihar, Andhra Pradesh and Madhya Pradesh.

Indian National Satellite Project - INSAT (1982)

As a part of INSAT project, ETV broadcasts were inaugurated and continued through terrestrial transmission from 15th August 1982 in Orissa and Andhra Pradesh. Later, other states namely Bihar, Gujarat, Maharashtra and Uttar Pradesh were covered under INSAT service using INSAT-1B in June 1983. As of today, these ETV programmes are offered in five languages - Oriya, Telugu, Marathi, Gujarati and Hindi- for a large population of primary school children. Programmes telecast in Hindi are being received in all Hindi-speaking states in the northern belt (IGNOU, 2000).

IGNOU-Doordarshan Telecast (1991)

The IGNOU-Doordarshan telecast programmes, designed mainly for Distance learners started in May 1991. Initially they were telecast on Monday, Wednesday and Friday from 6.30 to 7.00 am through the national network of Doordarshan with an aim to provide tele-counselling to students of open universities in remote areas. Owing to the encouraging response from viewers, the frequency of this project was increased to five days a week.

Statement of the Problem

The present study has been taken up to find out the level of awareness of ETV among the Diploma Level Teacher of Karur district. Hence, the problem of the study is stated as "ETV Awareness among the Diploma Level Teacher Trainees of Karur District.

Objectives of the Study

The main objectives of the study are:

1. To find out the awareness of ETV among the Diploma Level Teacher Trainees of Karur District.
2. To suggest measures to create, sustain and improve the Diploma level Teacher trainee's awareness of ETV.

Methodology

As the present study is descriptive by nature, normative survey technique was adopted. As many as 140 Student Teachers from two Diploma Level Teacher Training Institutions were chosen as sample using simple random sampling technique. A questionnaire, aimed at assessing their awareness of ETV used for the purpose of collecting data.

Operational Definitions of the Terms

The term 'ETV Awareness' includes information regarding Educational Television channels, the type of ETV programmes and the role of EDUSAT in Indian ETV experience and the knowledge of methods of utilizing ETV programmes for qualitative improvement in the teaching – learning process. The term 'Diploma Level Teacher Trainees' refers to the student Teachers with +2 qualification who are undergoing pre-service Teacher Training at Teacher Training Institutes and who would be qualified to teach at the primary level of school education.

Statement of the Problem

The present study has been taken up to find out the level of awareness of ETV among the Diploma Level Teacher Trainees of Karur District. Hence, the problem of the study is stated as "ETV Awareness among the Diploma Level Teacher Trainees of Karur District".

Objectives of the Study

The main objectives of the study are:

1. To find out the awareness of ETV among the Diploma Level Teacher Trainees of Karur District and
2. To suggest measures to create, sustain and improve the Diploma Level Teacher Trainees' Awareness of ETV.

Methodology

As the present study is descriptive by nature, normative survey technique was adopted. As many as 140 Student Teachers from Diploma level Teacher Training Institutes were chosen as sample using simple random sampling technique. A questionnaire, aimed at assessing their awareness of ETV used for the purpose of collecting data. The questionnaire was administered by the investigator in the respondents' respective institutions of work. The collected data were subjected to descriptive analysis.

Research Procedure

Selection of a particular research procedure depends on the objectives of research and suitability of the particular research procedure.

Sample for the Study

The present study aims to find out the ETV awareness among the Diploma Level Teacher Trainees of Karur District. As many as 140 (One hundred and forty) student teachers have been chosen to form the sample using simple random sampling technique. The student teachers who formed the sample were drawn from two Diploma Level Teacher Training Institutions, one Government and other Self financing.

Selection of the Tool

Data regarding general information, details of television viewing and educational television awareness were collected from Diploma Level Teacher Trainees of Karur District who formed the sample through the questionnaire.

Collection of Data

The ETV Awareness Questionnaire was administered to as many as 140 Diploma Level Teacher Trainees randomly selected from two Diploma Level Teacher Training Institutions.

Analysis of Data

The data obtained from the sample through the administration of the developed tool have been subjected to descriptive analysis in tune with the stated objectives. The data were analyzed through simple percentage analysis, this being descriptive research using normative survey technique. The analysis of data are presented in the form of tables below and further discussed after the tables.

TABLE. 3.1: Analyses of Sample in Terms of Gender, Locality and Medium of Instruction

Gender	No. of Candidates	%
Male	47	33.57
Female	93	66.43
Locality	No. of Candidates	%
Rural	102	72.86
Urban	38	27.14
Medium of Instruction	No. of Candidates	%
Tamil	130	92.86
English	10	7.14

The table (Table No. 3.1) presents the distribution of sample in terms of their gender, Level of Locality and Medium of Language. As seen in the table, out of the total sample (140 Student Teachers), 33.57 per cent are males and the remaining 66.43 per cent are females. From the table, it is clear that 72.86 per cent of the Student Teachers who formed the sample are Rural while the remaining 27.24 per cent hold Urban formed. As the table shows, among the 140 Student Teachers, 92.86 per cent belong to English medium and 7.14 percent belong to Tamil medium category.

TABLE. 3.2: Analyses of Sample in Terms of (Domicile) and Age

Locality	No. of Candidates	%
Day Scholar	65	46.43
Hosteller	75	53.57
Age	No. of Candidates	%
18-20	106	75.71
21-23	20	14.29
24-25	14	10.00

The table (table no. 3.2) presents the distribution of sample in terms of their Domicile and age. As evident from the table, 53.57 per cent of the Diploma Level Teacher Trainees who formed the sample are from Hosteller, while the remaining 46.43 per cent are from Day Scholar. As the table shows, among the total sample (140 Student Teachers), 75.71 percent are in the age group of 18-20, 14.29 percent are in the age group of 21-23 and the remaining 10.00 percent are in the age group of 24-26.

TABLE. 3.3: Analysis of Sample in terms of Frequency of TV Viewing

Frequency of TV Viewing	No. of Candidates	%
Daily	66	47.14
Alternate days	34	24.29
Once in a fortnight	26	18.57
Never	14	10.00

The above table (Table No. 3.5) presents the distribution of sample in terms of the frequency of television viewing. It is evident from the table that 47.14 per cent of the total sample (66 Student Teachers) has the habit of watching television daily; 24.29 per cent of the Student Teachers have the habit of watching television on alternate days;18.57 percent in a week; only (Teacher Trainees 10.00%) watch television never. There is none who does not have the habit of working TV.

TABLE. 3.5: Analysis of Sample in Terms of Length of TV Viewing

Length of TV viewing	No. of Candidates	%
1 – 3 years	39	27.86
4 – 6 years	31	22.14
7 – 9 years	23	16.43
More than 10 years	47	33.57

The table (table no. 3.6) represents the distribution of sample in terms of their length of TV viewing. It is evident from the table that all the 39 Student Teachers who formed the sample have 1-3 years of experience in 27.86 percent, 31 Student Teachers who formed the sample have 4-6 years of experience in 22.14 percent watching 23 Student Teachers who formed the sample have 7-9 years of experience in 16.43 percent and 47 Student Teachers who formed the sample have more than 10 years of experience in 33.57 watching following.

TABLE. 3.5: Analysis of Sample in Terms of their First Preference for Medium of Programs

Medium of Programme	No. of candidates	%
Tamil	125	89.29
English	13	9.29
Hindi	1	0.71
Others	1	0.71

The above table (Table No. 3.7) shows the distribution of students in terms of their first preference for medium of programs. It is evident from the table that a majority (89.29%) of the Student Teachers prefers to watch programs in Tamil. The next rating is for English programs, with 13 (9.29%) Student Teachers preferring it to others; as many as (0.71% Student Teachers) prefer to watch Hindi programs and 0.71% one Student Teachers to watch others programs.

TABLE. 3.6: Analysis of Response to Questions on ETV Awareness

Question No	Question	Response			
		Right	%	Wrong	%
1	ETV refers to Educational Television	92	65.71	48	34.29
2	Programs of Educational importance are available on ETV Channels	72	51.43	68	48.57
3	The Indian satellite for education is EDUSAT	108	77.14	32	22.86
4	An exclusive educational satellite has been launched by India Only	55	39.29	85	60.71
5	An ideal ETV Program is of ___________ duration.	24	17.14	116	82.86
6	ETV programs can be best used as Complementary to Class Room Teaching.	58	41.43	82	58.57
7	EDUSAT has paved the way for Radio Stations, Television Channels, Audio &Video conferencing and all the above.	72	51.43	68	48.57
8	ETV channels provide Video Programs with multimedia elements, video lectures and video recordings of classroom instruction.	64	45.71	76	54.29
9	ETV channels in India broadcast Programs of Educational Importance	40	28.57	100	71.43
10	The channel Gyandarshan caters to the academic needs of the students in School Education.	26	18.57	114	81.43

11	EMMRCs (Educational Multi Media Resource Centers) produce television programs on College Subjects.	52	37.14	88	62.86
12	EDUSAT is an Exclusive Educational Satellite	38	27.14	102	72.86
13	CIET (central Institute of Educational Technology) produces television programs on School Subjects.	35	25	105	75
14	On ETV channels, one can watch No Advertisement.	29	20.71	111	79.29
15	ETV channels in India are Co-coordinated by UGC-CEC.	22	15.71	118	84.29
16	Subject based Educational programs are available On other Doordarshan Channels also.	43	30.71	97	69.29
17	The channel Vyas caters to the academic needs of the students in Higher Education	72	51.43	68	48.57
18	ROT with regard to EDUSAT services refers to Receive only Terminal	24	17.14	116	82.86
19	Vyas Higher Educational is available Round the Clock on all Days.	42	30	98	70
20	UGC – CEC refers to UGC's Consortium for Educational Communication	47	33.57	93	66.43
21	ETV channels provide General Programs on Various Subjects; Syllabus based programs and Enrichment Programs.	33	23.57	107	76.43
22	The channel Ekalavya caters to the academic needs of the academic needs of the students in Technical Education.	49	35	91	65
23	SIT with regard to EDUSAT services refers to Satellite Interactive Terminal.	41	29.29	99	70.71

24	Through EDUSAT services, one can interact with other connected centers through video conferencing.	79	56.43	61	43.57
25	The life of EDUSAT with its full potential on the orbit is 12 years.	44	31.43	96	70.71
26	ETV Programs are best received when they are given through…..	54	38.57	86	61.43

*As the respondents were given the freedom to give multiple responses, data are presented separately.

Major Findings of the study

The following are the major findings that emerged from the descriptive analysis and interpretation of the data.

1. The ETV awareness of the Diploma Level Teacher Trainees of Karur District is below average
2. A majority of the women's students of Karur District are aware of the concept called Educational Television (ETV).
3. Only 50 percent of the samples of Diploma Level Teacher Trainees know about Educational TV channels and their programmes.
4. Only 75 percent of the Diploma Level Teacher Trainees who formed the sample are aware of EDUSAT as an exclusive educational satellite.
5. Only 39 percent of the Teacher Trainees are aware of the fact that India is the only country which has launched an exclusive satellite for education and the majority remaining is quite unaware of this fact.

Suggestions and Recommendations

Based on the above given findings and conclusions, the present study offers the following suggestions and recommendations:

1. Steps must be taken to increase the awareness, Educational Television and its potentials among the Student Teachers.
2. Watching ETV programmes should be included as compulsory component in the Diploma level Teacher Trainees programmes.
3. Interesting programmes should be telecast in the form of edutainment on ETV channels so as to gain the attention of the teaching-learning community.

Suggestion for Further Research

The findings of the present study open up a few areas for further investigation. They are as follows:

1. As this study has been taken up with only Diploma Level Teacher Trainees of Karur District as sample, studies with Diploma level student teachers and B.Ed level student teacher of other areas as sample may be taken up.

2. The same study can be replicated with more advanced statistical analyses in terms of gender, locality and other relevant variables.
3. Comparative studies can be taken up to compare the ETV awareness of the Diploma Level Student Teachers of Karur District with the Diploma Level Student Teachers of other Teacher Training Institutions.

Conclusion

Though it is specifically about the Diploma Level Teacher Trainees of Karur District, it presents a general view of the awareness of ETV among the Teacher Trainees by including the various aspects related to ETV in the purview of the study. The findings of the study would be of immense use to policy makers at the NCTE and state agencies of teacher education and curriculum planners for in-service training programmes.

❒

4

Development of Co.Animated Pack.for H.S.S.in Algebra and its Effectiveness:A Study

In a world of science and technology it is education that determines the level of property, welfare and security of the people. The development of human resources is dependent on the development of educational system. Now the world has witnessed four educational revolutions. Science and technology are used under educational technology. A more powerful animation technique often employed in games and educational software is cast-based animation, which is also known as sprite animation. Cast-based animation involves graphical objects that move independently of a background. Cast-based animation simulates movement using graphical objects that move independently of a background "A sprite is a graphical object that can move independently of a background or other objects."

Technology in education refers to the use of technological devices in educational system to facilitate effective instruction and evaluation through science and technological approach in education. According to the Council of Educational Technology (U.K), "Educational technology is the development, application and evaluation of systems, techniques and teaching aids to improve the process of human learning". According to Kulkarni "Educational technology may be defined as application of the laws as well as recent discoveries of science and technology to the process of education". Computer is an electronic device that can perform a variety of operations in accordance with a set of instructions called program. Computer can access and process data millions of times faster than human can. A computer can store data and information in its memory, process them and produce the desired results. The term 'Computer' is the origin from the Latin language word 'Compute' which means 'to calculate'.

WHAT IS ANIMATION?

Animation is the illusion of movement; probably the most surprising animated illusion is one that captured our attention long before modern computers-the television. When you watch television, you see lots of things moving around, but what you perceive as movement is really just a trick being played on your eyes.

TEACHING OF ALGEBRA

Algebra is one of the important branches of mathematics. In a true sense, it is a generalized arithmetic. Symbolism and Generalization are the two main characters, which may be observed in the structure and possesses of algebra. It helps in solving many complicated problems of arithmetic with much ease and simplicity. The students may see how they are helped by algebraic equations, formulae, and factorization etc. in the solution of such problems. Through its symbolism, algebra provides a sound language of clarity, brevity and accuracy to the mathematical thoughts and expression.

SIGNIFICANCE OF THE STUDY

In this cyber age, the unpredicted growth of computer animation a prominent role in teaching mathematics in the field of education, the growth of computer animation creates a major impact on the knowledge dissemination process and slowly it began to reach the status of a new source of information. Number of researchers has to be done in this part. Hence the researcher has chosen the development of computer-animated package for mathematics teachers and his area of study.

STATEMENT OF THE PROBLEM

"Development of Computer Animated Package for High School Students in Algebra and its Effectiveness."

DEFINITION OF THE TERMS

Development refers to the preparation of Computer Animated Package in Algebra for high school students with the help of Power Point.

COMPUTER ANIMATED PACKAGE

It is a package developed by the investigator for corresponding unit in Algebra for high school students by using Power Point.

ALGEBRA

Algebra is a branch of Mathematics, which deals with the parts of the equation. It is derived from the Arabic word 'Al-jabr' which means 'the' and 'reunion of broken words'. Addition, Subtraction, Multiplication, and Division of roots on the symbols and real numbers are called 'Algebric Equations'.

GENERAL OBJECTIVES

1. To develop computer animated package in Algebra for high school students.
2. To find out the effectiveness of computer animated package in Algebra for the high school students.
3. To find out the Computer self-efficacy of the experimental group students.
4. To find out the relationship between computer self-efficacy and achievement in mathematics of the experimental group students.

OBJECTIVES

1. To find out whether there is any significant difference between control and experimental group students in their gain scores.
2. To find out whether there is any significant difference between boys and girls of control and experimental groups in their gain scores.
3. To find out whether there is any significant difference between control and experimental group students in their gain scores for attainment of knowledge, understanding, application and skill objectives.
4. To find out whether there is any significant difference between control group boys and girls in attainment of the objectives knowledge, understanding, application and skill in their gain scores.
5. To find out whether there is any significant difference between experimental group boys and girls in attainment of the objectives knowledge, understanding, application and skill in their gain scores.

HYPOTHESES

1. There is no significant difference between control and experimental group students in there gain scores.
2. There is no significant difference between boys and girls of control and experimental groups in there gain scores.

3. There is no significant difference between control and experimental group students in their gain scores for attainment of knowledge, understanding, application and skill objectives.
4. There is no significant difference between control group boys and girls in attainment of the objectives knowledge, understanding, application and skill in their gain scores.
5. There is no significant difference between experimental group boys and girls in attainment of the objectives knowledge, understanding, application and skill in their gain scores

LIMITATIONS

The following are the limitation of the present study.

1. The researcher has selected only the topic ALGEBRA in mathematics for his study.
2. The two equivalent groups are formed on the basis of quarterly examination marks obtained in mathematics subject of the students but other factors are not considered.
3. The present study is limited to high school mathematics students.

METHODOLOGY

This study deals with the methods followed, tools used, sample and statistical analysis employed are described.

METHOD

The investigator has used experimental method for conducting the study. Experimentation is the name given to this type of educational research in which the investigator controls the educative factors to a student or a group of students subjected during the period of inquiry and observes the resulting achievement. Experimental research is the description and analysis of what will be or what will occur under carefully controlled condition.

SAMPLE

The investigator has selected DUDLEY Higher secondary school in Karur, Tamil Nadu for conducting the experiment. Both the control and experimental group students are selected in this school. There are 26 students in each group. Total sample consists of 52 students in forming the equivalent groups.

TOOLS

The following tools are used for data collection.

1. Computer animated package developed by the investigator.
2. Achievement test in mathematics developed by the investigator.

3. Computer self-efficacy scale developed by the investigator.

DEVELOPMENT OF COMPUTER ANIMATED PACKAGE

The investigator has prepared a Computer animated package on the topic 'Algebra' for the study. This topic is for the X standard mathematics students.

VALIDATION OF PACKAGE

The validation of computer animated Based Learning Package was done as follows:

- Expert's validation.
- Individual try out.
- Groups try out.

The blue print for the achievement test is given in the following table:

The Blue Print for the Achievement Test

S.no	Topics	Knowledge	Understanding	Application	Skill	Total
1	Polynomials	1,3,5,6,8,9	2,4,7	10.13	-	11
2	Algebric identity	12,14,16,17	19,21,22	11,15,20	18,24	12
3	Factorization	-	-	-	23,25	2
Total		**10**	**6**	**5**	**4**	**25**

ANALYSIS OF DATA

Statistical analysis is the process of collecting, analyzing and interpreting the numerical data and is one of the basic steps of research process. In this study the researcher uses Mean, Standard deviation and't' test to analysis the data.

Analysis of data means studying the tabulated material in order to determine inherent facts or meanings. It involves breaking down existing complex factors into simple parts and putting the parts together in new arrangements for the purpose of interpretation. A plan of analysis could make in advance before the actual collection of data. The collected data have been analyzed and the results are given as follows:

TABLE. 4.1: Level of Gain Scores of Control and Experimental Group Students

Group	Low		Moderate		High		Total
	N	%	N	%	N	%	
Control group	3	11.5	19	73.1	4	15.4	26
Experimental group	3	11.5	17	65.4	6	23.1	26

It is inferred from the above table that 11.5% of the control group students have low level, 73.1% of them have moderate level and 15.4% of them have high level of the gain scores. Among the experimental group students 11.5% of them have low level, 65.4% of them have moderate level and, 23.1% of them have high level of the gain scores.

TABLE. 4.2: Level of Gain Scores of Control and Experimental Group Boys and Girls

Group	Boys						Girls					
	Low		Moderate		High		Low		Moderate		High	
	N	%	N	%	N	%	N	%	N	%	N	%
Control group	2	14.3	10	71.4	2	14.3	1	8.3	9	75.0	2	16.7
Experimental group	1	7.1	8	57.1	5	35.7	2	16.7	9	75.0	1	6.67

It is inferred from the above table that 14.3% of the control group boys have low level, 71.4% of them have moderate level, and 14.3% of them have high level of the gain scores. Regarding the control group girls, 8.3% of them have low level, 75.0% of them have moderate level, and 16.7% of them have high level of the gain scores. It can be observed from the above table that 7.1% of the experimental group boys have low level, 57.1% of them have moderate level, and 35.7% of them have high level of the gain scores.

Regarding the experimental group girls, 16.7% of them have low level, 75.0% of them have moderate level, and 6.67% of them have high level of the gain scores.

TABLE. 4.3: Level of Gain Scores of Control and Experimental Group Students for Attainment of the Objectives

Objectives	Control group						Experimental group					
	Low		Moderate		High		Low		Moderate		High	
	N	%	N	%	N	%	N	%	N	%	N	%
Knowledge	0	0.00	23	83.5	3	11.5	8	30.8	14	53.8	4	15.4
Understanding	0	0.0	22	84.6	4	15.4	0	0.0	24	92.3	2	7.7
Application	3	11.5	17	65.4	6	23.1	3	11.5	19	73.1	4	15.4
Skill	0	0.0	25	96.2	1	3.8	13	50.0	10	38.5	3	11.5

It is inferred from the above table that 0.0% of the control group students have low level, 83.5% of them have moderate level, and 11.5% of them have high level of attainment of knowledge objective in their gain scores. Among the experimental group students, 30.8% of them have low level, 53.8% of them have moderate level, and 15.4% of them have high level of attainment of knowledge objective in the gain scores. The above table reveals that 0.0% of the control group students have low level, 84.6% of them have moderate level, and 15.4% of them have high level of attainment of understanding objectives in the gain scores.

Among the experimental group students, 0.0% of them have low level, 92.3% of them have moderate level, and 7.7% of them have high level of attainment the understanding objectives in the gain scores. It is inferred from the above table that 11.5% of the control group students have low level, 65.4% of them have moderate level, and 23.1% of them have high level of attainment the application objectives in the gain scores. Among the experimental group students, 11.5% of them have low level, 73.1% of them have moderate level, and 15.4% of them have high level of attainment the application objectives in the gain scores. It is inferred from the above table that 0.0% of the control group students have low level, 96.2% of them have moderate level, and 3.8% of them have high level of attainment the skill objectives in the gain scores. Among the experimental group students, 50.0% of them have low level, 38.5% of them have moderate level, and 11.5% of them have high level of attainment the skill objectives in the gain scores.

NULL HYPOTHESIS- 1

There is no significant difference between control and experimental group students in their gain scores.

TABLE. 4.4: Difference between Control and Experimental Group Students in their Gain Scores

Group (N = 26)	Mean	S.D	Calculated 't' value	Remarks at 5% level
Control group	2.73	1.13	9.46	Significant
Experimental group	6.15	1.46		

(At 5% level of significance the table value of 't' is 1.96

It is inferred from the above table that there is significant difference between control and experimental group students in their gain scores. That is, the experimental group students are better than the control group students in their gain scores. Hence, the developed computer animated package is effective for the 9th standard students.

NULL HYPOTHESIS- 2

There is no significant difference between boys and girls of control and experimental group students in their gain scores.

TABLE. 4.5: Differences between Gain Scores of Control and Experimental Group Boys and Girls

Group (N = 26)	Boys		Girls		Calculated 't' value	Remarks at 5% level
	Mean	S.D	Mean	S.D		
Control group	2.57	1.05	2.92	1.19	0.78	Not significant
Experimental group	6.64	1.39	5.58	1.32	1.99	Significant

(At 5% level of significance the table value of 't' is 1.96)

It is inferred from the above table that there is no significant difference between boys and girls of control group students in their gain scores, but there is significant difference between boys and girls of the experimental group students in their gain scores.

NULL HYPOTHESIS-3

There is no significant difference between a) control group boys and girls in attainment of the objectives knowledge, understanding, application and skill in their gain scores. Experimental group boys and girls in attainment of the objectives knowledge, understanding, application and skill in their gain scores.

TABLE. 4.6: Difference between Control and Experimental Group Boys and Girls in the Gain Scores for the Attainment of the Objectives

Objectives	Control group (N = 26)						Experimental group (N = 26)					
	Boys		Girls		Calculated 't' value	Remarks at 5% level	Boys		Girls		Calculated 't' value	Remarks at 5% level
	Mean	S.D	Mean	S.D			Mean	S.D	Mean	S.D		
Knowledge	0.29	0.45	0.58	0.86	1.08	NS	2.04	1.20	2.00	0.00	0.17	NS
Understanding	0.14	0.35	0.17	0.37	0.17	NS	0.43	0.77	0.33	0.47	0.32	NS
Application	1.79	0.86	1.67	1.18	0.29	NS	3.22	1.56	3.00	0.82	0.38	NS
Skill	0.36	0.48	0.50	0.65	0.63	NS	0.65	0.70	0.33	0.47	1.03	NS

(At 5% level of significance the table value of 't' is 1.96)

It is inferred from the above table that there is no significant difference between,

Control group boys and girls in their gain scores for attainment of knowledge, understanding, application, and skill objectives.

Experimental group boys and girls in their gain scores for attainment of knowledge, understanding, application, and skill objectives.

NULL HYPOTHESIS-4

There is no significant difference between experimental group boys and girls in their computer self-efficacy.

TABLE. 4.7: Differences between Experimental Group Boys and Girls in their Computer Self-Efficacy.

N = 26 Group	Boys		Girls		Calculated 't' value	Remarks at 5% level
	Mean	S.D	Mean	S.D		
Experimental group	109.86	5.25	116.75	4.49	3.61	Significant

(At 5% level of significance the table value of 't' is 1.96)

It is inferred from the above table that there is significant difference between experimental group boys and girls in their computer self-efficacy.

NULL HYPOTHESIS-5

There is no significant relationship between computer self-efficacy and achievement in mathematics of experimental group boys and girls.

TABLE. 4.8: Relationships between Computer Self-Efficacy and Achievement in Mathematics of Experimental Group Boys and Girls.

Group	Sex	Σx	Σy	Σx^2	Σy^2	Σxy	Calculated 'r' value	Remarks at 5% level
Experimental group (N = 26)	Boys	93	1538	645	169346	10258	0.403	significant
	Girls	67	1401	395	163809	7812	0.144	Not significant
	Total	**160**	**2939**	**1040**	**233155**	**18070**	**0.006**	**Not significant**

(For 24 df at 5% level of significance table the value of 'r' is 0.388)

It is inferred from the above table that there is no significant relationship between computer self-efficacy and achievement in mathematics of experimental group girls students, but there is significant relationship between computer self-efficacy and achievement in mathematics of experimental group boys students.

FINDINGS AND SUGGESTIONS

Findings

1. 15.4% of the control group students have high level of gain scores.
2. 23.1% of the experimental group students have high level of gain scores.
3. 14.3% boys and 16.7% girls of the control group students have high level of gain scores.
4. 35.7% boys and 6.67% girls of the experimental group students have high level of gain scores.
5. 11.5% of the control group students 15.4% of the experimental group students have high level of attainment of knowledge objective in their gain scores.
6. 15.4% of the control group students 7.7% of the experimental group students have high level of attainment of understanding objective in their gain scores.
7. 23.1% of the control group students 15.4% of the experimental group students have high level of attainment of application objective in their gain scores.

8. 3.8% of the control group students 11.5% of the experimental group students have high level of attainment of skill objective in their gain scores.
9. There is significant difference between boys and girls in their computer self-efficacy.

Suggestions for the Educational Administrators and the Teachers

On the basis of the findings, the following suggestions are offered.

1. Every school can use the computer-animated package for teaching mathematics.
2. Multimedia package must be used to teach the abstract topics in mathematics.
3. The teachers may be trained to prepare the computer-animated package for teaching mathematics.
4. Computer with LCD panel will be used in the classes in the school.
5. Students may be encouraged to use the educational usage in their home.

SUGGESTIONS FOR FURTHER RESEARCH

It is hoped that the present study can be extended for further research and few titles are given below.

1. Effectiveness of intelligent tutoring system for teaching mathematics to high school students.
2. Impact of computer animated package in learning mathematics for high school students.
3. Effectiveness of multimedia in inclusive education.
4. Effectiveness of whiteboard integrated method for teaching mathematics for normal and handicapped children.
5. The same study can be conducted in different subjects.

❐

5

Relationship between Parentaleducation and Student Achievement: A Study

Achievement testing plays a significant role in the teaching learning program in school. A class teacher constructs tests to work out the student's performance in a subject but majority of people in India are not in favor of present system of examination. Parents should understand the child's problem "It is much more important for parents to learn how to promote normal development than to master techniques for correcting distortions in the growth process". The research is restricted the secondary level, XI standard pupils, because it is crucial stage: After completion of this class, they will ready to write the public examination, there by paving the way to their future career. At this stage, the gender differences in Mathematics achievement and Influence of parents' education are to be analyzed. Hence the apt title "Influence of Parents' Education on Achievement in Mathematics" is chosen for investigation. A recent study exploring the relationships between level of parent's education, parent self-efficiency, children's academic abilities, and participation in a Head Start program found that level of parent education and program participation was significantly related to parental self-efficiency.

Because parent involvement parent education have been shown to be very important postured force in a child's life, one would expect that during such a critical and demanding phase the two more important in child development.

Home and school would increase the collaboration. Parent education often deals with values classification and the resolution of values and conflicts. For example, a parent who is resistant to offering a child certain freedoms may be acting from out dated belief system. Some group discussion and experimental activities might help parents to become aware of the source of the belief and to rich and understanding that certain belief needs to be updated. Too simply of parent's better communication skills, to teach they how to say limits would ignore deny their own serious problems.

Parent Education

The term "parent education" was defined as "instruction on how to parent". Parent education, as we will be using the term, refers to a systematic and conceptually based program, intended to impart information, awareness, or skill to the participants on aspects of parenting.

Achievement

Achievement testing plays a significant role in the teaching learning program in school. A class teacher constructs tests to work out the student's performance in a subject but majority of people in India are not in favor of present system of examination. Reason begin, these tests lack objectivity reliability and validity.

Need of the Study

As the investigator is a mathematics teacher she got interested to find out the possible reasons among the XI standard pupils, if there exists any gender differences in influences of parents' education level achievement in mathematics. The research is restricted the secondary level, XI standard pupils, because it is crazier stage: After completion of this class, they will be ready to write the public examination, there by paving the way to their future career. At this stage, the gender differences in Mathematics achievement and Influence of parents' education are to be analyzed. Hence the apt title "Influence of Parents' Education on Achievement in Mathematics" is chosen for investigation.

Relationship between Parental Educational Attainment and Student Achievement

Parents' play an important role in their children's learning. Aside from being actively involved in their children's education, parents also provide a home environment that can affect learning. Parents serve as a model for learning, determine the educational resources available in the home and hold particular attitudes and values towards education. Although it is difficult to examine the home environment of each student, the educational attainment and occupation of parents serve as an indicator of the values and resources with which parents create this environment. Given the wide range of student performance within each group, it is clear that the success of many students appears to be dependent on factors other than their parents' level of education.

Parent Involvement

"Parent involvement" and "Parent participation" are nebulous terms because there is an array of parent behaviors that these could include. To define parent involvement more operationally, Hoover-Dempsey, Bassler, and Brissie (1987) theorized a two-way breakdown into home-based activities (e.g., parent home tutoring) and school based parent involvement activities (e.g., parent volunteering, attendance at parent-teacher conferences).

Types of Parent Involvement

1. The traditional type of parent involvement type (the parent as audience or bystander-observer);
2. Parents as decision makers (as in School Advisory Committees or Parent Teacher Associations [PTAs] in which parents participate in school decision making activities);
3. Parents begin as classroom volunteers;
4. Parent as a paid paraprofessional or teacher's aide;
5. Parents as learners (e.g., participate in child development or parenting classes)
6. Parents as teachers of their own children at home.

Ways to Reach Parents

It is important for teachers to keep the lines of communication open. This involves not only sending regular newsletters and notes, but also obtaining information from parents. Teachers need to consider families' lifestyles and cultural backgrounds when planning home activities. Teachers can suggest appropriate programs and send home questions for families to discuss. This discussion can be carried over into class. Busy parents can include children in such everyday activities as preparing a meal or grocery shopping. Teachers can also suggest that parents set aside a time each day to talk with their children about school.

Statement of the Problem

The statement of the problem is "Relationship between Parental Educational and Student Achievement".

Objectives

The following are the objectives of the present study:

1. To find out the level of influence of parental education of higher secondary students.
2. To find out the significance difference between Influence of parents' education and achievement in Mathematics of higher secondary students.

Hypotheses

1. There is no significant difference between male and female higher secondary students with respect to Influence of parents' education.
2. There is no significant difference between rural and urban higher secondary students with respect to Influence of parents' education.
3. There is no significant difference among government, aided, private higher secondary students with respect to Influence of parents' education.
4. There is no significant difference between literate and illiterate fathers of higher secondary students with respect to Influence of parents' education.
5. There is no significant difference between literate and illiterate mothers of higher secondary students with respect to Influence of parents' education.

Limitation of the Study

Broadly speaking any study is impossible without limitation. Research studies in general will have limitation due to many factors. This study too has some limitations. It is the responsibility of the researcher to see that the study is conducted with minimum care in order to be reliable. However, the following limitations were unavoidable in the present study.

1. This study adopted survey method using questionnaires to collect data from respondents.
2. In this study, sample was confined to higher secondary students of various schools.
3. The sample respondents belong to age group between 15+ and 16+.

The generalizations of the study are to be viewed in the light of the above limitations that are Inherent in academic research.

Analogy

Most of the studies followed random sampling technique in the collection of data and the size of the selected samples ranges from 40 to 2400 samples. In majority of the studies data was collected from the school students and in few of the studies data was collected from the teachers and parents. In majority of the students the questionnaire, Opionnarrie Rating Scale developed by the investigator was utilized as a tool. Since all the reviewed studies were selected to influence of parent education, parent involvement, achievement in Mathematics among higher secondary students. In majority of the studies data was collected only from the school students. Mean, Standard deviation, t-test were the statistical technique followed in the majority of the students.

Methodology

Design of the Study

A research design however, is not a highly specific plan to be followed without direction. Rather, it is a series of guideposts to keep right direction. Thus, research design is the process of planning a research, choosing methods and procedures that can be expected to yield meaningful and most interpretable results.

TABLE. 5.1: Schematic Representation of the Research Design

S. No.	Type	Sources
1.	Nature of the Research	Survey research
2.	Tool Developed	Influence on Parental Education on Achievement in Mathematics
3.	Demographic variables	Students
4.	Variables	Boys, Girls (Gender) Rural, Urban (Locality) Government, Aided, Private (Type of the School) Literate, Illiterate (Father's educational qualification) Literate, Illiterate (Mother's educational qualification)
5.	Sampling Technique	Stratified Random sampling Technique
6.	Size of the sample	Students – 150 (Boys-75, Girls-75)
7.	Statistical Techniques used	Mean, Standard Deviation and 't' test

The present study belongs to survey stay Research. The Demographic variables used are Gender, Locality and Type of the school, Father's educational qualification and Mother's educational qualification. The tool "IPEAM" used in the study is 11th standard students for sample selection. Stratified Random sampling technique was followed in this study. Data were collected from 150 students and the statistical techniques mean, SD, 't' test and Average were used.

Blueprint

TABLE. 5.2: Blueprint for Achievement Test

Objectives	**Knowledge**			**Under standing**			**Application**			**Skill**			**Total**
Forms of questions / Content Unit	E	S.A	O	E	S.A	O	E	S.A	O	E	S.A	O	
Matrices	-	-	9	-	-	6	-	-	5	-	-	5	25
Vector Algebra	-	-	7	-	-	5	-	-	10	-	-	3	25
Sub total			16			11			15			8	50
Total (in %)	**32**			**22**			**30**			**16**			**100**

Pilot Study

Before administering the questionnaire to the actual sample, pilot study was conducted. The aim of pilot study is not only to test and refine the tools of research but also to force the nature of analysis and processing that may be needed at a later stage after a questionnaire was prepared. It was given a trial on small sample. This is necessary to know XI standard students whether they are meaningful and whether there is any ambiguity in thought or in the wording of questions.

Research Methods

The investigator followed Survey method as this study aims of eliciting the opinions of the XI standard students on achievement in Mathematics.

Tools

1. Achievement test with multiple choice questions
2. A questionnaire was prepared to get the information about matrix and vector Analysis in XI std students
3. Test method – Achievement test of 50 marks was conducted

Sample

A sample is a small proposition of a population selected for observation and analysis. By considering here the research which proposes to ascertain what is the normal or typical condition or practice at the present time". It is the only means through which opinions, attitudes and suggestions for improvement and such other data can be obtained. Survey studies help in contributing to other types of investigations and cover a large number of traits and characteristics of the group. A sample of 150 students of Higher Secondary level was selected from the following. Five difference higher secondary schools in Taluk of Namakkal district.

TABLE. 5.3: Distribution of Samples

S.No.	Variables	Category	No. of Samples
1.	Gender	Male	75
		Female	75
2.	Locality	Rural	79
		Urban	71
3.	Type of the School	Government	51
		Aided	50
		Private	49
4.	Fathers' Educational Qualification	Literate	91
		Illiterate	59
5.	Mothers' Educational Qualification	Literate	64
		Illiterate	86

Personal Data Sheet

The personal data sheet servers to collect personal information. Students were asked to write their name, gender, locality, age, name the school, type of the school, father's and mother's educational qualification.

Procedure

The questionnaire was prepared which included questions in XI standard Mathematics given to the students during extra periods. The students wrote the truthful answers. Further the classification and analysis of the results was carried out.

Questionnaire

A Questionnaire usually contains a series of well-planned and well-framed questions on the chosen topic. Which the subjects was asked to answer. "In general the word questionnaire refers to a device for securing answer questions by using a form which the responded fills himself". Barn, David and Johnson define questionnaire "A systematic computation of question that are submitted to a sampling of population from which information is desired"

Scoring Key

The three types of opionnarrie consist of questions. The total maximum scores 1 and minimum scores 0.

Statistical Techniques

For the analysis of data following statistical technique were adopted. They were,

1. Arithmetic Mean
2. Standard Deviation
3. 't'- test
4. 'f'- test

Arithmetic Mean

$$M = \frac{\sum fx}{N}$$

Standard Deviation

$$S = \sqrt{\frac{\sum fx^2}{N} - \frac{\left(\sum fx\right)^2}{N}} \times i$$

't'-test

$$t = \frac{m_1 - m_2}{\sqrt{\frac{SD_1^2}{N_1} + \frac{SD_2^2}{N_2}}}$$

'f' – test

Variance difference

$$f = \frac{Variance\ difference}{Variance\ within}$$

Delimitations of the Study

However, the following delimitations were unavoidable in the present study. The present investigation is confined to the students studying in Taluk, Namakkal District in Tamil Nadu. The study is confined only to a sample of 150 students from higher secondary schools located in rural and urban area. In this present study the investigator analyzed about the variables such as gender, locality, type of the school, father's educational qualification and mother's educational qualification.

Data Analysis

The purpose of present investigation is to study the influence of parental education on achievement in mathematics. The data for the study were collected from the students by means of a questionnaire. The analysis of data was attempted as per the objectives of the study. In the present study the data was anglicized using mainly the following techniques.

Hypothesis: 1

There is no significant difference between male and female higher secondary students with respect to influence of parents' education.

TABLE. 5.4: Significant Difference between Male and Female Higher Secondary Students with Respect to Influence of Parents' Education

Category	N	Mean	S.D.	't' value	Significance at 0.05 level
Male	75	44.83	17.62	4.51	No Significant
Female	75	57.5	16.73		

Table 5-4 examines the mean, standard deviation, 't' value and level of significance of male and female student's towards parents' education. The mean scores of male and female shows that there is significant difference in their influence of parents' education. The scores indicate that the two groups have difference. The 't' value of the group is 4.51 at 0.05 level. The calculated 't' value exceeds the tabulated value (1.98) at 0.05 level. Hence the null hypothesis is accepted.

Hypothesis: 2

There is no significant difference between rural and urban higher secondary students with respect to influence of parents' education.

TABLE. 5.5: Significant Difference between Rural and Urban Higher Secondary Students with Respect to Influence of Parents' Education

Category	N	Mean	S.D.	't' value	Significance at 0.05 level
Rural	79	43.72	14.64	5.86	No Significant
Urban	71	59.44	17.8		

Table 5-5 examines the mean, standard deviation, 't' value and level of significance of rural and urban student's towards parents' education. The mean scores of male and female shows that there is significant difference in their influence of parents' education. The scores indicate that the two groups have difference. The 't' value of the group is 5.86 at 0.05 level. The calculated 't' value exceeds the tabulated value (1.98) at 0.05 level. Hence the null hypothesis is accepted.

Hypothesis: 3

There is no significant difference among government, aided, private higher secondary students with respect to influence of parents' education.

TABLE. 5.6: Significance Difference among Government, Aided, Private Higher Secondary Students with Respect to Influence of Parents' Education

Category	N	Mean	S.D.	'f' value	Significance at 0.05 level
Government	51	51.97	23.16	1.56	Significant
Aided	50	39.7	10.6		
Private	49	66.31	15.75		

Table 5-6 examines the mean, standard deviation, 'f' value and level of significance of male and female student's towards parents' education. The mean scores of government, aided and private shows that there is significant difference in their influence of parents' education. The scores indicate that the two groups have difference. The 'f' value of the group is 1.56 at 0.05 level. The calculated 'f' value not exceeds the tabulated value (3.06) at 0.05 level. Hence the null hypothesis is rejected.

Hypothesis: 4

There is no significant difference between literate and illiterate fathers of higher secondary students with respect to influence of parents' education.

TABLE. 5.7: Significant Different between Literate and Illiterate Fathers' of Higher Secondary Students with Respect to Influence of Parents' Education

Category	N	Mean	S	't' value	Significance at 0.05 level
Literate	91	56.15	18.86	4.56	No Significant
Illiterate	59	43.63	14.55		

Table 5-7 examines the mean, standard deviation, 't' value and level of significance of male and female student's towards parents' education. The mean scores of literate and illiterate fathers' shows that there is significant difference in their influence of parents' education. The scores indicate that the two groups have difference. The 't' value of the group is 4.56 at 0.05 level. The calculated 't' value exceeds the tabulated value (1.98) at 0.05 level. Hence the null hypothesis is accepted.

Major Findings

From the present study the investigator came to the following findings:

1. There is no significant difference between male and female higher secondary students with respect to Influence of parents' education.
2. There is no significant difference between rural and urban higher secondary students with respect to Influence of parents' education.

3. There is a significant difference among government, aided, private higher secondary students with respect to Influence of parents' education.
4. There is no significant difference between literate and illiterate fathers of higher secondary students with respect to Influence of parents' education.
5. There is no significant difference between literate and illiterate mothers of higher secondary students with respect to Influence of parents' education.

Suggestions

1. Parents should monitor their children to use mass media/internet for necessary information.
2. Parents should educate their children in all their stages to overcome the teen age problems and help them out by providing their needs.
3. Parents should bear in mind that it is a temporary phase with most children. Some of the most destructive children have later on grown up to be among the most creatively constructive. Many of them outgrow this in time.
4. We should be very friendly with the child. Parents can instill the best of everything into their child. Try to improve yourselves to be his/her best companions. The child must have complete trust in you. Children usually love to try their hands at new things. Appreciate them and try a test their intelligence quotients (IQ).

Educational Implications

In summary, all parental influences derived from this study have implications for Mathematics. These influences, which include parents serving as role models of altruism, parental support for career goal achievement, high grade expectations, introductions to the positive aspects of teaching, parents involving children in hands-on learning experiences, and the creation of environments that nurture the discovery of vocational content are all important in creating interest in Mathematics.

Conclusion

The findings of the present study and earlier researches supported the notion that parents' education is one of the most important factors influencing child's achievement motivation. Highly educated parents have greater success in providing their children with the cognitive and language skills that contribute to early success in school. The relationship of parents' education to their children's achievement motivation in academic area is meditated by parents' beliefs and behaviors are likely to be influenced by their educational experiences and how these parental beliefs and behaviors actually influence children's achievement motivation in academic area. ❐

6

A Study of Family Relation and Job Satisfaction among Primary School Teachers

The teacher in the emerging Indian society has a vital role to play in the social reconstruction and in the transmission of wisdom, knowledge and experience of one generation to another generation. Children are the potential wealth of nation. They are always exposed to the information of the teacher. The roles of teachers are interrelated and inter-dependent. The teacher is required to play different roles and even the same role changes over the years. The teacher's role also differs from one stage of education to another. To illustrate this, it may be said that the role of teachers working in primary schools cannot be equivalent with that of their counterparts in higher education. Good teaching is of true love for teaching and students. In the teaching work the teacher should try to give a good start, because it creates interest and motivation in learning. It is rightly called that to make a good start is half way to win the battle. Good teacher continue to plan their work and prepare their lesson a fresh even if they teach the same subject to the same class for years.

The Successful running of any educational system depends mainly upon the teacher, the pupil, the curriculum and the facilities. Of these, the teacher is the most important one and is the pivot on whom the entire educational structure rests. As per our Indian ancestors, the teacher may be gleaned from the hierarchy of their gods: 'atrudev Bhava, Pitrudevo Bhava, Acharyadeva

Bhava; First, mother is god; second father is god; and Third, 'Acharya Bhava' or 'Guru', or the 'Teacher' is god. Further it is Said 'Guru Brahma Guru Vishnu Guru Devo Maheswaraha', which implies that the teacher is the creator, the sustainer and the ultimate liberator.

Teacher as a Protector of the Environment

Traditionally the teacher has been called the "Maker of History" "Social Engineer" and "Builder of the nation". The teachers of 21st century should be called as "Protectors of the environment" and "Saver of the environment", "Purifier of the environment" and Manager of the environment'.

Teacher as a Character Builder

The school plays a vital role in the moral development of the students and the most important agent in the school is the teacher. Nothing is more effective and helpful in moulding the child's moral behaviour. So the teacher has to set an example to the students.

Teachers as the Builder of the Nation

The teachers are rightly called as the "Builder of the Nation". Off all different factors, which build the young India in on emotional integrated nation, the role of the teacher is undoubtedly the most significant. The emotional integration of the Indian people is a challenge that cannot be ignored.

Determinants of Job Satisfaction

Many factors influence job satisfaction of employees. Review of research reveals the following important determinants of job satisfaction.

1. **Supervision**
   The first and foremost important determinants of job satisfaction are supervision and the style of leadership
2. **Job content**
   Another influential factor of job satisfaction is the job content refers to the factors such as recognition, responsibility, advancement, achievement etc., in the jobs employee perform.
3. **Specialization**
   The relationship between job specialization and job satisfaction is complex; specialization leads to greater efficiency in general, but at the sometime it lowers the job satisfaction to some people.

4. **Age**
   The Research reveals that old workers are satisfied workers. Job satisfaction usually trends to be high when people enter the work force.
5. **Race and Sex**
   Sex and Race also affect job satisfaction have been found that job satisfaction among male and females were equally affected by such determinants of job satisfaction as wages, prestige, and supervisory positions.
6. **Educational level**
   Keeping the occupational level as constant there is found a negative correlation between level of education of employees and their satisfaction. Dissatisfaction will be more when an educated person is employed in lower rungs.

Statement of the Problem

The statement of the problems is "A study of Family Relation and Job Satisfaction among Primary School Teachers in Trichy District".

Need of the Study

1. As family relationship and job satisfaction is the subject of psychology of human being, which depends on the working environment. Research efforts are needed more in this area.
2. Job satisfaction is that it consists of the total body of feelings about the nature of the job, promotion prospects, nature of supervision and so on.
3. An individual about his job if the sum total of influencing factors give rise to feelings of satisfaction, the individual has job satisfaction.
4. Changing any one of the, these influences will lead in the direction of job satisfaction or dissatisfaction depending upon the nature of change.
5. The standard of any educational institution, in turn, cannot rise beyond the level of its teachers. It would be rewarding, therefore, to identified the level of job satisfaction possessed by the school teachers.

Objectives of the Study

1. To find out the difference between family members of primary school teachers with respect to family relationship and job satisfaction.
2. To find out the difference between rural and urban of primary school teachers with respect to family relationship and job satisfaction.
3. To find out the difference between male and female, primary school teachers with respect to family relationship and job satisfaction.
4. To find out the diffidence between the ages, primary school teachers with respect to family relationship and job satisfaction.

5. To find out the difference between type of management of primary school teachers with respect to family relationship and job satisfaction.
6. To find out the difference between annual incomes of primary school teachers with respect to family relationship and job satisfaction

Hypothesis of the Study

1. There is no significant difference on the level of Attitude of family status and job Satisfaction on the basis of type of family.
2. There is no significant difference on the level of Attitude of family status and job Satisfaction on the basis of family member.
3. There is no significant difference on the level of Attitude of family status and job Satisfaction on the basis of Residence.
4. There is no significant difference on the level of Attitude of family status and job Satisfaction on the basis of Sex.
5. There is no significant difference between Attitude of family status and job Satisfaction on the basis of Age.
6. There is no significant difference on the level of Attitude of family status and job Satisfaction on the basis of Management.

Limitations of the Study

1. Data collection of this study restricted to Trichy district only.
2. Sample size confined to 100.
3. It focused on teacher's family relationship and job satisfaction among primary school teachers.
4. The study confines only Primary school level, so accurate generalization is not given.

Statement of the Problem

The statement of the problem is "A Study of Family relationship and job satisfaction among Primary School Teachers in Trichy District". Taking the objectives into consideration the following variables were selected for the present study.

Sample

A stratified random sampling technique was adopted for the selection of sample. 100 teachers were taken as sample for the study. The schools selected for this study is divided into different strata, namely Government, Government Aided and Matriculation.

Development of Questionnaire

Initially family relationship and job satisfaction questionnaire consisted of 65 'strongly Agree, agree, undecided, Disagree and strongly Disagree' type items selected on the basis of previous studies and following interviews with teachers and principals of higher secondary schools, Guide and teacher educators. These items were classified into four different aspects of family relationship and job satisfaction in teaching. These included,

1. Satisfaction with work,
2. Satisfaction with salary, security and promotion policies,
3. Satisfaction with institutional plans and policies, and
4. Satisfaction with authority including school management.

These 65 items so classified into five different aspects were given to a group of experts for their opinions and comments. These were also discussed with group of teachers of primary schools of Trichy district. In view of criticism and comments offered by experts and teachers, 17 items were altogether rejected, while others were modified or rewritten, sixty-five items were thus selected for the questionnaire. These items showed 100% agreement amongst the judges as related to family relationship and job satisfaction in teaching.

Item Selection

All the items were scored out to obtain the frequency distribution. 92 percent of the highest scores and 64 percentage of lowest score served as criterion groups (Kelly,1939). Discriminating value for each item was then determined. 82 items with discriminating value of 17 and 65 above were finally selected for the questionnaire.

It is emphasized that no item should be omitted and there is nothing 'right' or 'wrong' about these questions. There is no time limit for the questionnaire. However, it takes approximately 25 minutes to complete it.

S. No	Nature of Items	Statement
1	Positive	1,2,3,5,6,7,8,10,12,14,15, 16,18,19,21,22,24,28,29,31,32,33, 1,3,4,5,6,7,9,10,13,14,18,19,20,26, 27,28,29
2	Negative	4,9,11,13,17,20,23,25,26,7,30,34,35, 2,8,11,12,15,16,17,21,22,23,24, 25,30,

All the 39 items are positively worded. All these items are given a score of "5" for positive. The sum of these values gives the job satisfaction scores for the subject. The total score varies from 0 to 26, showing lowest job satisfaction to highest job satisfaction for the subject. The sample consisted of 100 male and female teachers or the primary schools teachers of the Trichy district.

Data Analysis and Interpretation

The next steps in process of research, after the collection of dates, are the organization, analysis and interpretation of data and formulation of conclusions and generalization to get a meaningful picture out of the raw information collected. The analysis and interpretation of data involve the objective material in the possession of the researcher and his subjective reactions and desires to be derived from the data. The total score of family relationship and job satisfaction of each teacher was taken to find out the level of job satisfaction possessed by each sub sample as well as total sample of the study. The maximum score that a teacher can get is 92% and the minimum is 64%. In the present study, the highest total score secured by a teacher was 299 and the lowest was 208.

For the purpose of a classification of the level of job satisfaction possessed by the Primary school teachers. The mean scores were used to identify the level of satisfaction of Primary teachers and to compare the sub-sample variation. The values of standard deviation were used distribution. The critical ratios were calculated to test the variable. The chi-square test of independence was applied for comparing the experimentally obtained results with those of two expected theoretically on the hypothesis of equal probable distribution.

Statistical Techniques Used

Statistical techniques serve the fundamental purpose of the Descriptive and Inferential Analysis. The collected data were tabulated, analysed and interpreted. The data were studied from many angles as far as possible to find our new facts. Following Statistical techniques were used in the study.

1. Mean and Standard Deviation
2. T- test
3. F- test

Hypothesis Testing

This hypothesis was tested by 'T' test and 'F' test.

The 'T' Test

The 't' test is a statistical test that allows to compare two means to determine the Probability that the difference between the means is a real difference rather than a change difference.

The test of significance of the difference between the two means is known as the't' test. It involves the ratio between experimental variance and the error variance.

$$t = \frac{M_1 - M_2}{\sqrt{\frac{SD_1^2}{N_1} + \frac{SD_2^2}{N_2}}}$$

The 't' value is compared with the value of 't' given in the 't' tables at the appropriate degree of freedom and at required level of significance. If the calculated 't' value then the difference between the sample means is significant at that level of significant.

'F' Test: The Variance Ratio Test

In the honor of statistician R.S. Fisher, the variance ratio test is named as 'F'- test. The main aim of this F – test is to determine the two independent estimates of population variance differ significantly.

Mathematically,

$$F = \frac{S_1^2}{S_2^2}$$

Where, $$S_1^2 = \frac{E(X_1 - X)^2}{N_2 - 1}$$

$$S_2^2 = \frac{E(X_2 - X)^2}{N_2 - 1}$$

$$F = \frac{\textit{Larger estimate of Variance}}{\textit{Smaller estimate of Variance}}$$

The 'F' Value is compared with the values of 'F' given in the 'F' at the appropriate degree of freedom and at required level of significance.

Differential Analysis

The section highlights differential studies identifying the difference between any two sub groups of the sample are discussed.

TABLE. 6.1: Showing the Composition of the Sample Selected for the Study Sex, Age, Management, Medium, Annual Income, Marital Status, School Distance, Type of Family, Family Member, Residence.

Variables	Categories	No. of respondents	Percentage
Sex	Male	45	45.0
	Female	55	55.0
Age	Below 25 years	30	30.0
	25 to 35 years	35	35.0
	Above 35 years	35	35.0
Management	Govt.	40	40.0
	Govt. Aided	30	30.0
	Matriculation	30	30.0
Medium	Tamil	70	70.0
	English	30	30.0

Annual Income	Below 75,000	30	30.0
	Above 75,000	70	70.0
Marital Status	Married	65	65.0
	Unmarried	35	35.0
Type of family	Nuclear family	60	60.0
	Joint family	40	40.0
Family members	Below 2	40	40.0
	2-5	30	30.0
	Above5	40	40.0
Residence	Rural	60	60.0
	Urban	40	40.0

The variable family relationship and job satisfaction has been categorized into low, average and high based on Quartiles.

Hypothesis-1

There is no significant difference on the level of Attitude of family status and job Satisfaction on the basis of type of family.

TABLE. 6.2: 't' Test Value for the School Teachers Attitude of Family Status and job Satisfaction on the basis of Type of Family

Type of family	N	Mean	SD	t-value	LS
Nuclear	60	78.15	6.16	0.98	NS
Joint	40	79.35	5.92		

The t-value is found to be 0.98 and it is less than the table value of 1.96. Hence it is not significant. Here null hypothesis is accepted and research hypothesis is rejected. To sum up nuclear and joint do not differ significantly in their attitude of family status and job Satisfaction.

Hypothesis-2

There is no significant difference on the level of Attitude of family status and job Satisfaction on the basis of family member.

TABLE. 6.3: 'F' Test Value for the School Teachers job Satisfaction and Attitude of Family Status on the basis of Family Member

Family member	N	Mean	SD	F-value	LS
2 member	30	78.70	6.34	0.19	NS
2-5 member	40	79.00	5.97		
Above 5 member	30	78.10	6.08		
Total	**100**	**78.63**	**6.06**		

The F-value is found to be 0.19 and it is less than the table value. Hence it is not significant. Here null hypothesis is accepted and research hypothesis is rejected. To sum up family member do not differ significantly in their school teachers attitude of family status and job Satisfaction.

Hypothesis-3

There is no significant difference on the level of Attitude of family status and job Satisfaction on the basis of Residence.

TABLE. 6.4: 't' Test Value for the School Teachers job Satisfaction and Attitude of Family Status on the Basis of Residence

Residence	N	Mean	SD	t-value	LS
Rural	60	79.08	6.65	1.04	NS
Urban	40	77.86	4.89		

The t-value is found to be 1.04 and it is less than the table value of 1.96. Hence it is not significant. Here null hypothesis is accepted and research hypothesis is rejected. To sum up rural and urban do not differ significantly in their attitude of family status and job Satisfaction.

Hypothesis-4

There is no significant difference between Attitude of family status and job Satisfaction on the basis of Age.

TABLE. 6.5: 'F' Test Value for the School Teachers Attitude of Family Status and job Satisfaction on the basis of Age

Age	N	Mean	SD	F-value	LS
Below 25	30	77.81	6.34	0.56	NS
26 to 35	35	78.60	6.46		
Above 35	35	79.41	5.43		
Total	**100**	**78.63**	**6.06**		

The F-value is found to be 0.56 and it is less than the table value. Hence it is not significant. Here null hypothesis is accepted and research hypothesis is rejected. To sum up age do not differ significantly in their school teachers attitude of family status and job Satisfaction.

Hypothesis-5

There is no significant difference on the level of Attitude of family status and job Satisfaction on the basis of Management.

TABLE. 6.6: 'F' Test Value for the School Teachers Attitude of Family Status and job Satisfaction on the basis of Management

Management	N	Mean	SD	F-value	LS
Government	40	80.58	6.60	3.73	0.05
Aided	30	77.70	4.02		
Private	30	76.97	6.47		
Total	**100**	**78.63**	**6.06**		

The F-value is found to be 3.73 and it is greater than the table value. Hence it is significant at 0.05 levels. Here null hypothesis is rejected and research hypothesis is accepted. To sum up management differ significantly in their school teachers attitude of family status and job Satisfaction.

Hypothesis-6

There is no significant difference on the level of attitude of family status and job Satisfaction on the basis of Annual Income.

TABLE. 6.7: 't' Test Value for the School Teachers job Satisfaction and Attitude of Family Status on the basis of Annual Income

Annual Income	N	Mean	SD	t-value	LS
Below 75,000	30	76.97	6.47	1.73	NS
Above 75,000	70	79.34	5.78		

The t-value is found to be 1.73 and it is less than the table value of 1.96. Hence it is not significant. Here null hypothesis is accepted and research hypothesis is rejected. To sum up below 75,000 and above 75,000 do not differ significantly in their attitude of family status and job Satisfaction.

Findings and Conclusion

The problem chosen for this study was an investigation into the Family relationship and job satisfaction of primary school teachers in relation to the above variables. The variables considered in the study were Gender, age, Management, medium, income, marital status, school distance, type of family. Family member and residence (Rural and Urban) were identified keeping the different aspects of the present study in view.

Findings

1. The obtained value of t-test was less than the table value for the variable "Type of Family" has not differs significantly in their family relationship and job satisfaction.
2. While considering the variable "Family Member" the F-value was less than the table value, so it has not differ significantly is their family relationship and job satisfaction.

3. The calculated value of t-test for the variable "Residence" was less than the table value so it has not differ significantly in their family relationship and job satisfaction.
4. From the result of the t-value we obtained is 0.80, which is less than the table value of 1.96, so the variable "sex" was not differ significantly in their family relationship and job satisfaction.
5. The calculated F-value is less than the table value, so the variable "Age" was not differ significantly in their family relationship and job satisfaction.
6. From the above F-test calculation the value obtained was greater than the table value, so the variable "Management" has differ significantly in their family relationship and job satisfaction.

Recommendations

The above variables were considered for this study, from these variables which has not affect significantly in their family relationship and job satisfaction of the primary school teachers of Trichy district, were type of family, family member, and residence (Rural and Urban), Gender, age, medium, income, marital status.

Two variables are considered from the calculation, which significantly affect the primary school teachers of Trichy district, were "Management" and "School Distant". So the teachers who get employment in Government and Aided School are highly job satisfied and with Family relationship. But the primary school teachers are not highly satisfied with the variable "Management". For better solution, the primary school teachers try to get employment for Government and Aided school, which are within twenty kilometers.

Suggestions for Further Research

In the light of the present research and its results, it is suggested to undertake the following studies in a methodical way and with wider approach in order to bring into focus the variables and areas, which were not incorporated in this study.

1. Studies may be taken up to study the family relationship and job satisfaction to teachers working in secondary schools and higher secondary schools.
2. Studies may be taken up to identify the psychological factors that contribute for effective teaching and job satisfaction also.
3. Studies may be taken up on experimental basis to enhance the job satisfaction of teachers at all level.

Conclusion

The following are the conclusions drawn from the present study on family relationship and job satisfaction of primary school teachers. The conclusions are analyzed and discussed in order to utilize them in enhancing the effectiveness and family relationship and job satisfaction.

1. The primary school teachers were having good family relationship and job satisfaction respective of the type of family, family member, and residence (Rural and Urban), Gender, age, medium, income, marital status.
2. The teachers working in government and aided primary schools has high job satisfaction and good family relationship. There is no difference in the level of both. But Self Finance school teachers are not satisfied with their jobs. And schools distant were also affecting the primary school teachers of all management.

❐

7

Study on Secondary School Women Teacher's Problems in Tamilnadu

The contribution of the large band of some extraordinary men, philosophers, educators, leaders of the reformed Hindu Church was immense as it lifted women from the substratum of society, from sub-human existence to a level of relatively greater human dignity. As the freedom movement became mass-based, women's participation in increasing numbers became visible ad they began raising some basic questions about their rights. Before entering into an analysis of women teachers and their association with the teaching vocation it is of much use to be aware of women empowerment which has had its impact both in private and national life.

In the early 19th century, the modern (western) system of education was founded under the East India Company charter of 1813. But in these scheme women's education found no place. It was due to the fear of the British that women's education was a taboo in the Hindu religious and social context. The expectation was the women folk would receive education from the men folk in a manner and measure the society approved it. Women's education, thus, had the character of dependability and a matter purely private. It was left to the sheer discretion of the individual families. It is noted that better scales of pay commensurate with rising costs of living, is the first priority to attract good teachers and to maintain morale in the teaching profession. Though the teaching profession has become a marketable commodity due to spread of education and multiplication of schools and colleges and demand of teachers the quality and leadership of teachers are wanting in great measure.

WOMEN EMPOWERMENT AND ITS IMPACT

Involvement of women in public life such as educators is an element that transforms the status of women, as well as family relationships, the socialization of children and the organization and division of work. The presence of women in the public area has profound effects on traditional practices, attitude and values on a rigid division of work along gender lines and on stereotypes derived from this division. Yet these women teachers have their own quota of problems to face in their daily professional routine. They have many problem-challenges which they ought to face while they carry on their career and have to overcome them successfully so that they do justice in fulfilling their professional obligations. The problems are related to physical, occupational, familial, social and psychological aspects.

NEED FOR THE STUDY

In the present era, Indian women constitute an important segment of the total labour force that causes national development. Exposure of women to formal education and participation in paid labour force bring change in their role and status. Today women are in a situation where they have to take multiple roles and responsibilities. This study on the problems of working women teachers in Trichy Taluk, Trichy District is empirical in character based on primary data collected from the ground. As such the questionnaire method was followed for the present study. The required details were collected by distributing the questionnaire to the women teachers working in this area. Accordingly, the procedures adopted constituted the following steps:

The subject of the study was working women teachers from 103 primary and middle schools in Trichy Taluk in the age group 25 to above 50. 106 primary & middle school women teachers scattered over 105 schools (primary & middle) in this area were selected randomly for investigation. All the teachers investigated were government employee teachers.

STATEMENT OF THE PROBLEM

The present study is entitled "Investigation on The Problems of Women Teachers in Trichy Taluk, T.N."

SCOPE OF THE STUDY

The scope of the present research is limited to the study of the problems of the women teachers in the schools of Trichy block. The samples of study are engaged in teaching in the Government Primary and Middle Schools in the Union. All the respondents have completed school education or above. In addition to that all the teachers have completed secondary level teachers training programme, a basic teacher eligibility qualification. A small percentage who have B.Ed. qualification had been promoted to be middle school teachers in the Taluk. The present study attempts to probe into the problems of working teachers from five different angles.

SPECIFIC OBJECTIVES

The specific objectives of this investigation are to study the physical, familial, occupational, social and psychological problems of working women with respect to

1. Age - below 30yrs, 31-40 yrs, 41-50 yrs, above 51 yrs
2. Community - OC, BC, MBC, SC/ST
3. Educational qualification - School, College
4. Co-workers - Male/Female / Both

HYPOTHESES

The following hypotheses are formulated for the study and presented in the null form:

1. There is no significant difference among the mean scores of physical problems, occupational problems, familial problems, social problems and psychological problems of women teachers of different age groups.
2. There is no significant difference between the mean scores of physical problems, familial problems, occupational problems, social problems and psychological problems of women teachers with respect to marital status.
3. There is no significant difference among the mean scores of physical problems, familial problems, occupational problems, social problems and psychological problems of women teachers belonging to different community groups.
4. There is no significant difference between the mean scores of physical problems, familial problems, occupational problems and psychological problems of Hindu and Christian respondents.
5. There is no significant difference between the mean scores of physical problems, familial problems, occupational problems and psychosocial

problems of women teachers having school and higher educational qualifications.

6. There is no significant difference between the mean scores of physical problems, familial problems, occupational problems and psychosocial problems of women teachers having occupational status of Secondary Grade training or B.Ed.
7. There is no significant difference between the mean scores of physical, familial, occupational, social and psychological problems of women teachers having male and female co-workers.

SCHOOLS AND TEACHER POPULATION

The union has 103 government Primary and Middle schools. The teacher population has grown steadily over the years. Now about 350 primary & middle school teachers are working in Trichy Block, among them 238 are women teachers.

SAMPLE

As noted previously primary and middle school women teachers constituted the sample of the study. The total sample came nearly to the number of total female teachers in the union.

PROFILE OF WORKING WOMEN TEACHERS RESPONDENTS

1. Age

There is a statutory limit in practice either for minimum or maximum age for a woman teacher in governmental service. There is variation of women teachers in the present study, ranging from below 30 years to above 50 years. The details of percentage distribution of working women teachers by the age group are furnished below:

TABLE. 7.1: Working Women Teachers by Age Group

Age Groups (years)	Number of Respondents	Percentage
Below 30	14	13.21
31 – 40	82	77.36
41 – 50	04	03.77
Above 50	06	05.66
Total	**106**	**100**

It can be observed from Table 1 more than 75% of the respondents were in the age group of 31- 40 years. A meager 13% of the women teachers were in the age group of meager 3.77% were in the age group of 41-50.

2. Community

TABLe. 7.2: Distribution of the Respondents According to Community

Community	Number of Respondents	Percentage
OC	10	09.44
BC	62	58.50
MBC	14	13.20
SC/ST	20	18.86
Total	**106**	**100.00**

The above table indicates that women belonging to BC were about three-fifth and they were more in employment than the other communities. The OC and MBC respondents were nearly equal in number and were below about the fifth each. SC/ST respondents were one-fifth.

3. Educational Background

For the present study, the women teachers who had completed secondary school education and women teachers with college education working in primary and middle schools in Trichy Taluk area, were considered.

TABLE. 7.3: Education level of the Respondents

Educational Backgrounds	Number of Respondents	Percentage
School Level	66	62.26
College Level	40	37.74
Total	**106**	**100.00**

It can be observed from the above table that out of the total respondents, nearly three-fifths of women teachers had secondary school level education and about two-fifths of the women teachers had completed college education.

4. Co-Workers

The colleagues of the women teachers may be men, women or both. The rapport and relations with them may enhance the working capacity.

TABLE. 7.4: Sex of the Colleagues

Colleagues	Number of Respondents	Percentage
Male	16	15.10
Female	24	22.64
Both	66	62.26
Total	**106**	**100.00**

It can be observed from the above table that nearly one-seventh of the respondents had male colleagues. Nearly two-sevenths of the women teachers worked with female colleagues and nearly four-seventh of the respondents had both male and female colleagues. It shows that the traditional taboos are slowly loosening the grip over Indian working women.

TOOL

After the discussion the investigator finalized the variables and developed a tool for the investigation. The question contained statements in Tamil with sometimes simple equivalents in English in brackets. The tool was developed to study the physical, occupational, familial, social and psychological problems of working women. The tool comprised of three parts. Part I had demographic variables such as Age, Marital Status, Religious Faith, Community, Educational Level, Occupational Status, Co-workers, Boss, Family Type, Generation Category and Years of Service to collect the general information about the respondents. The second part was with five subdivisions namely physical problems, familial problems, occupational problems, social problems and psychological problems. Part II of the tool was a three point scale-'Yes', 'Sometimes' and 'No' with positive and negative statements. The value for the choice is as follows:

'Yes' responses 3 points for positive items & 1 for the Negative
'Sometimes' responses 2 points for positive items & 2 for the Negative
'No' responses 1 point for positive items & 3 for the Negative

VALIDITY AND RELIABILITY

The investigator constructed a tool for the present study and sent to nine experts to test its content validity. The experts were two scholars in economics and seven scholars in education. The scholars suggested corrections such as avoiding value-laden words, using simple words, framing questions on sensitive areas carefully, arranging statements coherently etc. On the basis of the suggestions necessary corrections were made and the content validity and the reliability of the tool were established.

The tool was administered on all female teachers of primary and middle schools in Trichy Taluk. But only 106 of the teachers cooperated in the study. The incompletely filled questionnaires were identified by the name of the school of the respondent and taken back to the concerned respondents and the filling up was completed. They were quantified, tabulated and analyzed using appropriate statistics. The same tool was administered to the same respondents after a gap of two months. The reliability co-efficient were derived with test-retest method and they were as follows:

PILOT STUDY

The pilot study was started by the investigator by personally administering the tool to 35(10%) respondents in Trichy Taluk. All of them were working Government primary and middle school women teachers. Some questionnaires were not filled in completely. There were 106 questionnaires with complete responses. The data collected were quantified, tabulated and analyzed using appropriate statistics. Each item in the questionnaire was found to be important and retained for the final study.

STATISTICAL TECHNIQUES EMPLOYED

The collected data were quantified, tabulated and fed into computer. The programmes appropriate to the objective of the study were made use of in the analysis of data. The following statistical techniques were employed:

- Critical ratio test and
- Analysis of variance

ANALYSIS AND INTERPRETATION OF DATA

The data collected on the problem of working women teachers in Elementary schools in Trichy Taluk were subjected to statistical analysis. The correlation analysis, the analysis of variance and the Schaffer Test were employed to know the significant difference in Physical, Occupational, Familial, Social and Psychological problems of working women teachers on the basis of demographic variables. The findings and conclusions were arrived on the basis of the values of the subsequent test for the integration of all the problems.

(Here, only three hypotheses analysis mentioned out of seven)

TABLE. 7.5: There is no Significant Difference among the mean Scores of Physical Problems, Occupational Problems, Familial Problems, Social Problems and Psychological Problems of Women Teachers of Different Age Groups.

Problems	Source of Variance	Sum of Squares	df	Mean of Squares	'F' Value	Table Value	Result at 0.05 level
Work and Health	Between	11.9728	3	3.9909	0.5614	2.698	N.S.
	Within	725.1666	102	7.1095			
Work and Body condition	Between	89.4025	3	29.8008	2.1938	2.698	N.S.
	Within	1385.5662	102	13.5840			
Physical problem (Total)	Between	65.7579	3	21.9193	0.6938	2.698	N.S.
	Within	3222.4876	102	31.5930			

The data shown in the above table reveals that there are no significant difference among the mean scores of the sub component of the physical problem-work, health, work & body condition and physical problem with reference to the age of the teachers. Hence the null hypothesis is accepted.

TABLE. 7.6: There is no Significant Difference among the mean Scores of Physical Problems, Familial Problems, Occupational Problems, Social Problems and Psychological Problems of Women Teachers belonging to Different Community Groups.

Problems	Source of Variance	Sum of Squares	df	Mean of Squares	'F' Value	Table Value	Result at 0.05 level
Conveyance	Between	2.5894	3	086.31	0.6537	2.698	N.S.
	Within	134.6740	102	1.3203			
Working condition	Between	16.0576	3	5.3526	0.9014	2.698	N.S.
	Within	605.6640	102	5.9379			
Benefit scheme	Between	12.7725	3	4.2575	4.8262	2.698	Sig
	Within	89.9798	102	0.8822			
Sex Problem	Between	13.8841	3	4.6280	8.2707	2.698	Sig
	Within	57.0761	102	0.5596			
Co-worker	Between	0.6049	3	0.2016	0.6400	2.698	N.S.
	Within	32.1349	102	0.3150			
Boss	Between	11.9331	3	3.9777	8.3409	2.698	Sig
	Within	48.6429	102	0.4769			
Occupational Problems (Total)	Between	59.4944	3	19.8315	1.3456	2.698	N.S.
	Within	1503.2482	102	14.7377			

It is obvious from the figures given in the above table that the occupational problems like conveyance, working condition and support from co-worker were not significant to women teachers with respect to different age groups. It was also clear that there is significant difference in sub components like benefit, scheme, sex problem and boss with respect to age. Hence the null-hypothesis is rejected.

TABLE. 7.7: There is no Significant Difference between the mean Scores of Physical Problems, Familial Problems, Occupational Problems and Psychosocial Problems of Women Teachers having School and Higher Educational Qualifications.

Problems	Source of Variance	Sum of Squares	df	Mean of Squares	'F' Value	Table Value	Result at 0.05 level
Income and Social Status	Between	4.4644	3	1.4881	1.4270	2.698	N.S.
	Within	106.3694	102	1.0428			

Support From Family	Between	37.8660	3	12.6220	6.9532	2.698	Sig
	Within	185.1587	102	1.8153			
Family Relationship	Between	69.3804	3	23.1268	3.3221	2.698	Sig
	Within	710.0766	102	6.9615			
Decision Making	Between	5.0936	3	1.6979	1.7121	2.698	N.S.
	Within	101.1514	102	0.9917			
Familial Problems **(Total)**	Between	229.2628	3	76.4209	3.9765	2.698	Sig
	Within	**1960.2514**	**102**	**19.2182**			

The above table discloses that there were significant differences among the mean scores of the sub components of the familial problems, support from family, relationship with family members and decision-making with reference to age.

RESULT AND DISCUSSIONS

These problems are basically of five types namely physical, occupational, familial, social and psychological. These problems are studied in terms of age, community, educational, qualification, co-workers, generation and years of experience of the respondents. The respondents were classified on educational level as school and college education. Regarding psychological problems teachers of school level educational qualification faced more problems than their counterparts. On the whole, there was no significant difference in physical, occupational, familial and social problems between the two categories.

COMMUNITY AND PROBLEMS OF OMEN TEACHERS

Women teachers such as OC, BC, MBC, SC & ST were taken for study. There was significant difference among SC & ST and other community respondents with respect to physical problem while no such significant difference was noted regarding occupational, physical, social and psychological problems. The respondents taken for study had female or both male and female colleagues. There was no significant difference indicated between the mean scores of the sub-dimensions of the problems regarding physical, psychological and social with reference to co-workers and significant difference was manifested regarding familial and occupational problems. Respondents having female co-workers felt more occupational and psychological problems.

RECOMMENDATIONS

There are various teacher-career improvement programmes organized at Central Government and State Government levels for elementary and middle school teachers. Such programmes concentrate only on the teacher-taught and teaching methodologies. But there are no specific efforts taken to holistically study the various crippling problems of the teachers that handicap total performance in the class-room environment. Efforts should be taken to organize down-to-earth programmes by highly qualified and trained professional resource personnel to make teachers become aware of their personality inadequacies and of those pertaining to physical, occupational, familial, social and psychological aspects for continual corrections. As recommended a holistic and systematic approach of this kind will produce total performance in teachers making education a total success.

Conclusion

The above findings pertaining to the problems of women teachers in Trichy Taluk enabled the investigator to arrive at the following conclusions:

1. Age, and independent variable inference the problems of the women teachers. The magnitude of the problems varied with the age. The higher the age the greater was the intensity of the problems.
2. Concerning the classification of the community the SC & ST groups occupies the lowest rung of the social stratification ladder, even after very many years of independence. The Governmental polices helped only a microscopic minority of this category to throw off the shackles of social discrimination and have social vertical mobility.
3. As to the educational level of the respondents considered for this investigation, i.e. School and college level, significant repercussions were identified. Teachers who have completed school studies grappled with more problems of all types than their counterparts.
4. Regarding the co-workers of the respondents of this investigation, the female colleagues were found to be the troubleshooters in the work spot.
5. With reference to years of service and problems of working women irrespective of the number of years of service, whether less or more, all the respondents encountered problems from different angles. It may be concluded that problems of any nature are inherent for women teachers in different scores.

❒

8

Awareness of Virtual-Learningn among Student-Teachers

The use of education in ICT means tremendous addition in our knowledge or information. Through the medium of Information Technology, a number of novel concepts were brought forth in the field of education. Along with the concepts, newer and newer challenges are kept before teachers. As a result, a teacher's role has not remained limited only up to the class room, but scope has expanded and it got transformed into global classroom. This is because of the introduction by ICT include novel concept such e-learning, M-learning, distance learning, virtual classroom and soon. The Goal of Virtual –Learning is to provide access to that part of the population who would not able to attend an physical campus, for reason such as distance –where students live too far from a physical campus to attend regular classes; need for flexibility –some students need flexibility to study at home whenever it is convenient for them to do so.

NEED FOR THE STUDY

Nowadays the College Students are communicating through technology such as Web pages-e- mail, and another networked sources. The Researcher understood that Virtual -Learning are the one of the important learning tool for various levels of education. So the Researcher is motivated to know the level of awareness among student teachers towards Virtual-learning. Therefore they coined the topic as " Awareness towards Virtual-Learning among student-Teachers in Colleges of Education".

OBJECTIVES OF THE STUDY

The objectives of the study are i) to measure the level of Awareness towards Virtual-Learning among Student- Teachers in Colleges of Education. ii) to measure the level of significant difference on the Awareness towards Virtual-Learning among Male and Female, Arts and Science Student- Teachers and Student- Teachers and UG and PG qualified Student- Teachers.

HYPOTHESES

The Null hypotheses were formulated to realize the above objectives.

NATURE OF THE RESEARCH

As the study aimed to measure the Awareness towards Virtual-Learning among Student- Teachers in Colleges of Education, it is a Normative Survey Research.

DEVELOPMENT OF TOOL

The investigator developed a Two Point Scale to measure the Awareness about Virtual-Learning among Student- Teachers in colleges of Education. There were 26 statements in this questionnaire. The developed questionnaire was given to the Teacher Educators and Experts who are involved in Education field to verify whether the instruments are really aimed to measure the Awareness about Virtual learning among Student- Teachers. Their valuable suggestions were incorporated. Moreover, test – retest method was followed to find out the reliability among the Student- Teachers. The obtained 'r' value 0.81 shows that the tool is highly valuable. Thus the Validity and Reliability of the tool were established.

SAMPLE SELECTION

Investigators used Systematic Random Sampling Technique and selected Student- Teachers from 3 Self Finance Colleges of Education in Tiruchirappalli District as samples. The Tool was given to the 110 Student- Teachers. The filled – in questionnaires were received from them were 101. The total samples have been classified further on the basis of Gender, Subject, Locality and Qualification.

TABLE. 8.1: Sample Distribution

S.No	Category	Size
1.	Male Female	35 66
2.	Arts Science	62 39
3.	Urban Rural	25 76
4.	UG PG	72 39

DATA ANALYSIS

Thus the data collected in this manner undertake analysis by using different statistical technique. Mean and SD were calculated for each Variables to calculate 't' values which is the test of significance of the difference between two Means.

TABLE. 8.2: Mean and SD of the Student- Teachers towards Awareness towards Virtual-Learning among Student- Teachers with different Category.

Sl.No	Components		N	Mean	SD
1.	Total		101	78.37	11.43
2.	Gender	Male Female	35 66	78.57 78.26	11.36 11.56
3.	Subject	Arts Science	62 39	78.23 78.60	11.19 11.96
4.	Locality	Urban Rural	25 76	77.23 78.74	11.59 11.43
5.	Qualification	UG PG	72 29	77.88 80.77	11.54 10.88

From the above Table 8.2 it is revealed that the total Mean Scores of Awareness towards Virtual-Learning among Student- Teachers in Colleges of Education is 78.37. This reveals Awareness towards Virtual-Learning among Student- Teachers was good among Student- Teachers. Moreover the minimum score is 60.47 and the maximum score is 80.77.

TABLE. 8.3: Significance Difference on the Mean Scores of Male and Female Student- Teachers towards Awareness on Virtual-Learning

Category	N	Mean	SD	t value	Remarks
Male	35	78.57	11.36	0.23	NS
Female	66	78.26	11.56		

NS: Not Significant S: Significant

From the above Table 8.3 it is understood that the't' value 0.23 shows that there is no significant difference at 0.05 level. On observing the Mean Scores among Male and Female Student- Teachers with respect to the Awareness towards Virtual-Learning are similar. Hence the framed Null Hypothesis is accepted.

TABLE. 8.4: Significance Difference on the Mean Scores of Arts and Science Student- Teachers towards Awareness about Virtual-Learning

Category	N	Mean	SD	t value	Remarks
Arts	62	78.23	11.19	0.5	NS
Science	39	78.60	11.96		

NS: Not Significant S: Significant

The't' value 0.5 from the above Table 8.4 shows that it is not significant at 0.05 level. The result shows that the Mean Scores among Arts and Science Student- Teachers with respect to the Awareness towards Virtual-Learning are similar. Hence the framed Null Hypothesis is accepted.

TABLE. 8.5: Significance Difference on the Mean Scores of Student- Teachers who were living in Urban and Rural Area towards Awareness on Virtual-learning

Category	N	Mean	SD	t value	Remarks
Using android Mobile	25	77.23	11.59	0.48	NS
Not using android Mobile	76	78.74	11.43		

NS: Not Significant S: Significant

From the above Table 8.5 it is seen that the 't' value 0.48 is not significant at 0.05 level. These results show that the Mean Scores of Student- Teachers who were living in Urban and Rural area with respect to the Awareness towards Virtual-Learning are similar. Hence the framed Null Hypothesis is accepted.

TABLE. 8.6: Significance Difference on the Mean Scores of Student- Teachers who were Under Graduates and who were Post Graduates Student Teachers Awareness on Virtual-Learning

Category	N	Mean	SD	t value	Remarks
UG	84	77.88	11.54	6.14	S
PG	17	80.77	10.88		

NS: Not Significant S: Significant

The table shows that their exist the 't' value 6.41 indicates there is a significant difference between UG and PG student teachers among the awareness of Virtual-Learning. The table also shows that PG Student –Teachers having higher Mean Score than UG Student –Teachers. Hence the framed Null Hypothesis is accepted.

FINDINGS

The salient findings of the study are i) All the Student- Teachers are having good Awareness on Virtual-Learning. ii) Male and Female, Arts and Science, who are living in Urban and Rural area or Not shows similar level of Awareness on Virtual-Learning. iii) PG Student –Teachers having higher Mean Score than UG Student –Teachers.

CONCLUSIONS

The Student- Teachers are having higher awareness towards Virtual-Learningit is a positive trend because this higher awareness towards Virtual -Learning indicates tremendous improvement in the learning. The result shows that Gender, Group studied, Locality are Not the determining factors for the awareness of Virtual-Learning. But the results show that PG Qualified Student-Teachers were having higher Mean Scores than the UG Student -Teachers. This may be due to PG qualified Student- Teachers are frequently using internet or other learning source for Virtual learning..

EDUCATION IMPLICATIONS

The results of the present study shows that Student-Teachers are having higher awareness towards Virtual-Learning therefore the various Educational Organizations may produce the various education packing systems facilitate virtual learning. Then only the Students shows more interest towards virtual learning. The Government and Authorities should emphasise the importance of Virtual- Learning among the Students even in the school level.

❐

9

An Assessment of Edu Digital Skills among Teachers in Namakkal District

Teacher is an ideal personality whose knowledge and skill play a major role in the development of the nation to the global standard education in general and tapping the potentialities of students to the maximum extent in particular. Teachers are expected to learn forever to withstand the innovations in teaching and updating the knowledge and widen the clarity of the conceptual framework of the subject of specialization too. Unless and until the teachers prepared to meet the requirements and challenges, the dream and purpose of education will not be fulfilled. Nowadays the system of education has assumed the character which involves more students' participation and student centric which is highly enabled through the application of various educational technologies. Edu - digital skills is considered prerequisite for all teachers teaching for nursery to doctorate scholars. 21st century school curriculum has been enriched to meet the demands of world requirements of quality. Communication, collaboration, critical thinking, problem solving, creativity, invention, information and technology literacy and self direction will facilitate the achievement of aims and objectives of education. Teachers of 21st century are expected to equip themselves with modern technology application in teaching and learning process. A paradigm shift has happened to meet the demands of gen y and z learners which require innovative, explorative and interesting approach in teaching and learning. The curriculum will need withstand the futuristic vision for the global scenario. At this juncture the teachers of today should be enthusiastic to update their knowledge and skills forever in order to keep young to the youngest generation whom they meet and it may also be emphasized greatly as the professional ethics. This study has been attempted to assess the knowledge and skills of teachers in the field of information and communication technology which a teacher necessarily possess in the digital world.

Educational Digital Skills

It is mentioned that in order to thrive in a digital economy, students will need digital age proficiencies. It is important for the educational system to make parallel changes in order to fulfill its mission in society, namely the preparation of students for the world beyond the classroom. Therefore, the educational system must understand and embrace the following 21st century skills within the context of rigorous academic standards.

The 21st Century Literacy Summit (2002) contends that "the explosive growth of technology in every aspect of society offers us a unique opportunity to engage our citizens in economic and civic life" The report further states that to take advantage of this opportunity, we must continually acquire and develop new knowledge and skills. Summit participants noted "Information and communication technologies are raising the bar on the competencies needed to succeed in the 21st century, and they are compelling us to revisit many of our assumptions and beliefs" The sheer magnitude of human knowledge, world to technology necessitates a shift in our children's education - from plateaus of knowing to continuous cycles of learning. Therefore, policymakers and educators alike must define 21st century skills, highlighting the relationship of those skills to conventional academic standards. As they do so, they must also recognize the need for multiple assessments to measure these skills within the context of academic standards, evaluating their application to today's technological and global society.

Technological Literacy

Demonstrate a sound conceptual understanding of the nature of technology systems and view themselves as proficient users of these systems. Understand and model positive, ethical use of technology in both social and personal contexts. Use a variety of technology tools in effective ways to increase creative productivity. Use communication tools to reach out to the world beyond the classroom and communicate ideas in powerful ways. Use technology effectively to access, evaluate, process and synthesize information from a variety of sources. Use technology to identify and solve complex problems in real-world contexts have been considered as Technological Literacy

Information Literacy

Before Accessing Information one should determine what is known and what is needed for problem solving, identify different sources of information, including text, people, video, audio, and databases and prioritize sources based on credibility and relevance. When Accessing Information one need identify and retrieve relevant information from sources and use technology to enhance searching. Revise information-gathering strategies that prove to be in effective when understands how information retrieved does or does not address original problem, evaluate information in terms of credibility and know what are the social, economic, political, legal, and ethical issues that may impact it to facilitate to use technology for evaluation. After Information is extracted, using retrieved information to accomplish a specific purpose, present information clearly and persuasively by using a range of technology tools and media and evaluate the processes and products of these activities have here been considered essential to assure one to be Literate in information.

Global Awareness

Global awareness is knowledge about the connectedness of the nations of the world historically, politically, economically, technologically, socially, linguistically, and ecologically and understand that these interconnections of positive benefits and negative consequences too. The ability to recognize, analyzes, and evaluates major trends in global relations and the interconnections of these trends with both their local and national communities. Participate in the global society by staying current with international news and by participating in the democratic process.

Objectives of the Study

To find the level of Edu-digital skill among school teachers and find whether there is significant different exist among them in relation to their personal variables such as sex, Age, Educational Qualification, Area of Residence, Management of the Institution, Subject of Specialization and the Location of the School.

Research Question

What is the level of educational digital Skills of School Teachers? Is there any Significant Difference Exists among them with respect to their Personal Variables?

Research Methodology

A Normative Descriptive Method of study has been attempted to assess the level of Educational Digital Skills among the School Teachers in Namakkal District

Population, Sample and Sampling Technique of the Study

All teachers who teach in school education are the population of the study and the sample of the study has been chosen from teachers work in Namakkal district only and the sample was taken by stratified random sampling technique which consists of 250.

Tools and Technique of Data Collection

A tool consisted of 24 items related to some basic skills necessary for adopting computer enabled teaching technology, using internet connection which will benefit students to gain knowledge, understand the concept better, improve the critical thinking, problem solving ability, creativity and to enhance their communication skill and appropriate application of the knowledge gained for the betterment of himself and to the society. The scope of this study extent all teachers who teach in the classroom from kindergarten to plus two levels. The questionnaire has dimensions of using the computer for retrieving useful information via internet, knowledge about various search engines, and preparation of effective PowerPoint materials, video clippings, software package application, audio recording, connecting to virtual classroom and the facilities to publish the students works in internet. Knowledge and the application of MS word, Excel format, mobile for teaching and learning purpose and the ability to set ready LCD, mike and arrange show in the smart classroom and the application of social media in education have also been taken for assessing.

Scoring Procedure & Statistical Tools Used

The Questionnaire used in the study has five point scale of the level of skill of the respondents in relation to their digital skill hence it has five options of known very well, known, moderately known, known little and Unknown which scored as 5, 4,3,2 and 1 respectively.

SPSS package has been used to analyze the data and the percentage analysis and the differential analysis have been used to describe and infer the details pertaining to the research question formulated for the study.

TABLE. 9.1: An Analysis of Edu Digital Skills among Teachers in Namakkal District

Items	Very well Known		Well Known		Moderately Known		Known Little		Unknown		Total
	F	%	F	%	F	%	F	%	F	%	
Information Retrieval	41	16.4	59	23.6	62	24.8	75	30	13	5.2	250
Power point preparation	52	20.8	67	26.8	53	21.2	60	24	18	7.2	250
Efficient use of Windows operating system	35	14	48	19.2	75	30	81	32.4	11	4.4	250
Connecting to the Online Teaching of World Classroom	15	6	20	8	39	15.6	116	46.4	60	24	250
Skill in make it work well of LCD mike screen view	15	6	26	10.4	77	30.8	114	45.6	18	7.2	250
Knowledge about E learning material preparation	21	8.4	15	6	27	10.8	129	51.6	58	23.2	250
Account in social networking sites like Face-book, twitter	22	8.8	36	14.4	74	29.6	12	4.8	106	42.4	250
Using of videos and computer games in teaching	19	7.6	29	11.6	55	22	85	34	62	24.8	250
Application of Virtual classrooms and chat rooms in teaching and learning	13	5.2	18	7.2	17	6.8	56	22.4	146	58.4	250
Application of documentary film in deliverance of the instructional objectives	51	20.4	60	24	41	16.4	31	12.4	67	26.8	250
Using of web- Camera in virtual interaction	16	6.4	41	16.4	27	10.8	71	28.4	95	38	250
Application of white Board in teaching	25	10	16	6.4	19	7.6	43	17.2	147	58.8	250
Safety and security issues in using webmail	17	6.8	39	15.6	90	36	70	28	44	17.6	250
Security Challenges in instant messaging	15	6	35	14	78	31.2	98	39.2	24	9.6	250
Application of iPod and tables in teaching	11	4.4	23	9.2	67	26.8	80	32	69	27.6	250
Application of Video conferencing for teaching and learning	32	12.8	24	9.6	71	28.4	90	36	33	13.2	250
Application of YouTube	49	19.6	86	34.4	55	22	62	24.8	38	15.2	250
Application of Flicker & Picasa	19	7.6	25	10	62	24.8	104	41.6	40	16	250
Application of mobile phone for transferring data of video	21	8.4	27	10.8	80	32	90	36	32	12.8	250
Application of mobile phone for transferring data of voice	22	8.8	33	13.2	76	30.4	81	32.4	38	15.2	250

Items	Very well Known		Well Known		Moderately Known		Known Little		Unknown		Total
Application of mobile phone for transferring data of text	187	74.8	46	18.4	3	1.2	9	3.6	5	2	250
Assessment of students performance through online	25	10	52	20.8	58	23.2	105	42	10	4	250
Application of learning Management System - LMS	11	4.4	21	8.4	37	14.8	57	22.8	15	6	250
Application of Video-recording	17	6.8	26	10.4	51	20.4	78	31.2	78	31.2	250

Majority of teachers have necessary in Skill and knowledge in the application of MS office, Mobile technology in teaching and learning, information retrieval system from online resource centre but the majority teachers have moderate and least knowledge about e-content preparation, application of social media, and security issues in web mails, various learning management system and efficient use of ICT in teaching

TABLE. 9.2: Significance of Difference in Edu-Digital Skill of Teachers

Demographic Variables	P Value	Level of Sig.
Sex	0.153	NS
Area of Residence	0.104	NS
Location of the School	0.214	NS
Teaching Experience	0.098	NS
Educational Qualification	0.521	NS
Management of the School	0.021*	S
Subject of Specialization	0.001**	S

There is no significant difference exist among the respondents in their Educational digital skill in relation to their personal variables of Sex, Area of Residence, Location of the School, Teaching Experience and their educational qualification. But the statistical report of analysis shows that there is significant difference exist among the sample in relation to their management of the school and their subject of specialization.

Educational Implications

1. Teacher Education curriculum should emphasize the ICT enabled education in B.Ed program
2. Workshops need to be conducted for B.Ed program in the practical application of ICT and training program can be organized for E- content preparation

3. Orientation and Refresher courses for the teachers in schools should be conducted frequently to enable teachers to facilitate them in the efficient use of ICT in teaching and learning environment
4. Collaborative Approach should be made in integrating ICT in education

Conclusion

Teachers are the forerunner of all developments and growth of the nation and the world; they play a significant role in bringing desirable outcome in the world with their adaptability and their ever learning behavior of updating knowledge and skills in any field. No technology can replace the teacher in any period of time but the teacher needs possess skills in the application of technology which facilitate desirable educational outcome in the field of education.

❒

10

Impact of Computer Technology on Achievement in Tamil Language

Education is facing significant challenge in preparing students and teachers for our future' knowledge-based' society at a time when most teachers are trained to use them. In recent years, educational access to digital information and communications technology (ICT), tools, applications, networks, and media worldwide has grown dramatically. The digital ICTs are not single technologies, but combinations of hardware, software, media, and delivery systems. These four dimensions- integration of multiple media, interactivity, flexibility of use, and connectivity- distinguish digital ICTs form previous technologies. Because of these differences, educators are finding powerful new ways to integrate digital ICTs into the curricula. Now days, computers are used in the classroom as a support system to improve the teaching-learning process. It is also possible to use the computers to teach new skills or concepts, give remedial teaching, provide for enrichment of learning, promote creative thinking and problem solving etc.

NEED FOR THE STUDY

ICTs have the potential to be used in support of these new educational methods, enabling students to learn by doing. ICTs can make it possible for teachers to provide students with self paced, self-directed problem-based or constructivist learning experiences, as well as to test student learning in new, interactive, and attractive ways that may better assess the depth of their understanding of content and processes. New technologies in teaching and learning causes change in the environment of education. Education now changes from teaching environment to learning environment i.e., teacher based to student based education. The student based education curriculum should be need based to develop motivation, skillful, joyful in learning, learning life-long by students themselves etc which can be achieved by the utilization of computers inside the classroom. From the experiences it is found that CAI has become a powerful tool for the teacher in his instruction. The teacher has a changing role to play in the new technological society and goes out of his conventional assignment of traditional method of teaching alone. It is significant that CAI directly interacts with students individually and with the teacher. In the teaching learning process the teacher employs CAI as a tool to enhance the quality of the instruction The investigators were motivated by the various developments in the methods of teaching and have taken up the experimental study .The effect of computer Technology in teaching Tamil language among standard X students" to know how much extent computer Technology influences the effect of learning among the X standard students.

OBJECTIVES OF THE STUDY

The major objective of the study is to measure the effect of tutorial mode of CAI on Achievement in Tamil Language among Standard X students. The specific objectives are,

1. To measure the effect of tutorial mode of CAI on Achievement in Tamil Language over the Traditional Method of Teaching (TMT) with respect to Locality of the students.
2. To measure the effect of tutorial mode of CAI on Achievement in Tamil Language over the TMT with respect to their parents' Education and Qualification.
3. To measure the effect of tutorial mode of CAI on Achievement in Tamil Language over the traditional method of teaching TMT with respect to Parents' Locality , Education and Occupation.

METHODOLOGY

The study belongs to experimental research based on cause and effect relationship. The cause is the utilization of tutorial mode of Computer software to teach and the effect is the achievement in the subject Tamil Language by the X standard student.

SAMPLE

The size of the sample was 60 students of standard X. Two groups of students were selected in which the control group was taught through the tutorial mode of CAI and the Experimental Group through the traditional method of teaching.

VARIABLES

The two variables used were Dependent and Independent variables. Dependent variable was the achievement in Tamil Language (Grammar chapter) and the Independent variable was the readymade software available utilized for tutorial mode of teaching.

TOOL DEVELOPMENT

An Achievement Test in Tamil Language with 25 items in the chapter Grammar with multiple choices is prepared to measure the performance of the students. It is shown to the PG teachers in language and Teacher Educators for subject and content validity. All the appropriate procedures were followed to prepare the achievement test.

COLLECTION OF DATA

The prepared ATS is administered between two groups of the students of standard X belonging to Sri Vidya Mandir Matriculation Higher Secondary School, Rasipuram in Tamilnadu. Control groups was taught through the Traditional method of teaching and the Experimental group was taught through Tutorial mode of CAI making use of the ready-made CD utilizing the computer laboratory. Pre-test was conducted before the Treatment and the post test was conducted after the Post-test.

STATISTICAL TECHNIQUE

The administered questionnaire is scored and the achievements of the students in their pre and post tests were tabulated. The Mean and Standard deviation were calculated. To find out the significant difference between the variables, t' value were found.

DATA ANALYSIS

The results are presented in the following tables.

TABLE. 10.1: t' Test for the Mean Scores of the Total Students

S. No.	Category	No	Pre Test		Post Test		't' Value	Remarks
			Mean	SD	Mean	SD		
1.	Control	30	50.40	13.60	68.13	14.31	4.92	SD
2.	Experimental	30	52.13	13.21	75.45	12.76	6.96	SD

From the above table (1) it is obvious that there is Significant Difference in the mean scores of the Control and Experimental group in total at 0.05 levels. The Mean values of control and experimental groups reveal that treatments of traditional and computer assisted instruction made significant difference on achievement in Tamil Language. It is interpreted that both methods are good.

TABLE. 10.2: t' Test for the Mean Scores of the Experimental Group in the Pre and Post- Tests

S. No.	Category		Pre Test		Post Test		't' Value	
1.	Locality	Rural	53.71	16.04	71.71	13.54	2.08	SD
		Urban	47.50	9.45	65.00	14.64	2.89	SD
2.	Parents Education	XII	48.50	14.74	65.75	13.14	2.51	SD
		UG	49.33	5.47	69.33	19.21	1.02	NSD
		PG	46.00	8.49	74.00	2.83	0.82	NSD
		Others	58.00	16.92	71.33	15.88	0.58	NSD
		Agriculture	51.43	19.79	66.29	13.23	0.75	NSD
3.	Parents Occupation	Business	51.42	17.35	61.14	18.14	0.47	NSD
		Govt EMP	50.66	7.30	73.66	10.71	3.12	SD
		Others	46.00	13.26	67.00	17.39	0.98	NSD

From the table (2) there is significant difference in the mean scores of the students with respect to the Locality either they belong to Rural or Urban at the 0.05 level between control and experimental. Similarly on analyzing the mean scores of the students with respect to Parents Education there is Significant Difference only in the students whose parents' education is up to XII level at 0.05 levels. There is no significant difference in the mean scores of the students whose parents education is UG, PG and other Professional degrees in spite of their gain in the mean scores between the pre and post test were more.

While comparing the mean scores of the students with respect to their Parents occupation there is no significant difference in the mean sores of the students whose parents are employed in Government at 0.05 levels. There is no significant difference in the mean scores of students whose parents' occupation are Agriculture and other Professional.

THE FINDINGS OF THE ABOVE STUDY ARE LISTED AS FOLLOWS

1. There is Significant Difference in the mean scores between pre and post tests in Tamil Language of the Control and Experimental groups in total.
2. In the Control group,
    - There is Significant Difference in the mean scores of the control group with respect to Locality for both Rural and Urban students.
    - There is Significant Difference in the mean scores of the students with Parents' education up to XII level and there is No Significant Difference with respect to the students whose parents are Graduates, Post- Graduates and Professionals etc.
    - There is No Significant Difference in the mean scores of the students whose parents' occupations are Agriculture, Business and Other professionals. But there is Significant Difference in the mean scores of the students whose parents are Government Employed.
3. In the Experimental group
    - There is significant difference in the mean scores of the students with respect to the Locality either they belong to Rural or Urban.
    - There is No significant difference in the mean scores of the students whose parents education is UG, PG and other Professional degrees and there is Significant Difference in the students whose parents' Education is up to XII level.
    - There is no significant difference in the mean scores of students whose Parents' occupations are Agriculture, other Professional and there is Significant difference in the mean sores of the students whose parents Occupation is business and Government Employment

Conclusion

From the findings of the study it is evident that computer assisted Instruction has made significant effect on achievement irrespective of rural and urban schools they study. The special characteristics of immediate feedback, individualized instruction, animated presentation, colorful representation of the content may be the reasons for the significant difference on the achievement of the students. In some of the category, significant achievement was not observed. This is to be probed further. It concluded that, as significant difference was observed. All the students may be encouraged to utilize the potentiality of the computer and software facilities.

❐

11

Edu-Digital Skill among Higher Secondary Students

Education, the foremost weapon for social reform, is now under the forces of change. Newly formed branches of knowledge and techniques of education facilitate the physical, mental and emotional development of the learners. Schools have an unavoidable role in acquainting the students with the nature of changing field of education and in making necessary changes in the instructional techniques. In the modern world of technological innovations, all educational institutions are trying to improve their quality in terms of facilities and academic outputs.

Scientific knowledge is exploding every day. Knowledge available to mankind today is emerging in the form of science and technology. There is no limit or end to the accumulation of scientific knowledge. It also satisfies the intellectual thirst of human beings. Science education is a bridge between science and education, using psychology. It links the most powerful concepts of science to the growing minds of children through active experimental pedagogy. Science education plays a prominent role in Indian educational system. It has, as its objective, the aim of providing individual learners a firm grasp of the concepts and processes of science as also to impart the ability to use scientific method of problem-solving. As a result of it, every aspect of human civilization has been influenced to a very great extent.

The present world is the world of science and technology. Science is the most inexhaustible storehouse of knowledge. Continuous advances in scientific and technological research have led to the growth and greater application of science in contemporary society. The purpose of science education is to give individuals a firm grasps of the concepts and processes of science and to develop scientific attitude, scientific reasoning, problem solving ability and scientific temper and to impart them the ability to use the scientific method to other situations in life. Hence science education has been included in school curriculum at all levels. It is however necessary that science teaching be impressive so as to inculcate its values in young minds.

The increasing importance of informatics in day-to-day life has resulted in the emergence of computers in education at the international level. The worldwide recognition gained for the importance of computers has compelled educationists to revise the existing curricula to include informatics components. Even the developing countries have realized that unless they invest heavily in computer education, they will be left behind in the informatics revolution. Computers are being used in education to prepare the children for the informatics future by training them in programming and related skills for work in the informatics industry. They are also being used as educational aids to improve children's skills in academic subjects at all levels of education. Introduction of computers in education has brought out changes in the content and methods of education. However, lack of resources remains one of the main obstacles to the introduction and development of informatics in education in a large way in developing countries.

The most striking innovation in the field of educational technology is the use of computers. Computer is included in the hardware approach of educational technology. It is one of the machines of automation in teaching and learning and is used for presenting individualized instruction. The main objective of teaching through computer is to provide the needed flexibility for individualizing the educational process. It meets the specific needs of the student in a way in which is almost impossible to do in a face-to face student-teacher relationship.

Computers should have a major role in the teaching-learning process. Computers have become an essential class room tool for the acquisition, analysis, presentation, and communication of data in ways that allow students to become active participants in research and learning. The computers offer students very important resources for learning concepts through simulations, graphics, sound, data manipulation and model building. Computers can improve scientific learning and facilitate communication of ideas and concepts.

There are three roles for computer in education. First, it functions as a tutor for students by presenting material, evaluating responses, and depending on the basis of the evaluation, deciding what to present next. Second, it is a tool that helps students perform calculations, analyze data, keep records, or write papers. Third, it functions as tutee by having told what to do through programming.

A computer program can be designed to create models for experimental purpose. Students, that particularly in higher education, have the benefits of using computer as a computational tool. They learn a programming language and write a program to solve some of their course work problems treating the computer as an aid in much the same way as a slide rule or a set of mathematical tables. Computers are capable of giving almost instant feedback, tirelessly, no matter how many learners 'get it wrong' and it is equally well known that human tutors have limited value when it comes to learners repeatedly getting things wrong.

REVIEW OF LITERATURE

Dalacosta et al. (2009) developed and studied the effectiveness of Multimedia **application with animated cartoons in teaching science in elementary education.** The results of the study provide evidence that the use of animated cartoons significantly increases the young students' knowledge and understanding of specific science concepts, which are normally difficult to comprehend and often cause misconceptions to them.

Jian Hu et al. (2009) investigated the effects of introducing a software program, named the Dental 3D Multimedia System (D3DM), into the education of a group of junior dental students in their preclinical practice. One group received their training program in the traditional way, unassisted by 3D technology. The second group received their training program in the traditional manner, but also used the D3DM to supplement their education. The results showed that the D3DM-assisted group achieved higher scores and also indicated that the usage of 3D multimedia PC software had a positive impact on several aspects of subjects' performance.

Kanmani and Radha (2009) studied the Effectiveness of CAI package in basic electronics teaching. There was a significant difference between the control and the experimental group students in attainment of knowledge level, understanding level, and application level objective in the gain scores. Hence, the experimental group students were better than the control group students in attainment of knowledge level, understanding level, and application level objective in the gain scores. It was inferred from the finding that the experimental treatment is effective to the students.

Korakakis et al. (2009) made a study on the **"3D visualization types in multimedia applications for science learning for 8th grade students in Greece".** The aim of the study was to determine whether the use of specific types of visualization (3D illustration, 3D animation, and interactive 3D animation) combined with narration and text, contributes to the learning process in science courses. The results indicated that multimedia applications with interactive 3D animations as well as with 3D animations do in fact increase the interest of students and make the material more appealing to them.

She, Hsiao-Ching and Chen, Yi-Zen (2009) examined how middle school students constructed their understanding of the mitosis and meiosis processes at a molecular level through multimedia learning materials presented in different interaction and sensory modality modes. The dependent variables included subjects' pre-test, post-test, and retention-test scores, showing their understanding of mitosis and meiosis process at molecular level. The results of the study showed that the group which used multimedia learning material has a greater amount of visual attention and consistent with their long term retained learning than the group which did not use the same. This study adds empirical evidence of a direct correlation between the length of eye fixation behavior and the depth of learning. Moreover, it provides insight into the multimedia effect on students' cognitive process through the use of eye fixation behavior evidence.

Anboucarassy (2010) studied the effectiveness of Multimedia in Teaching Biological Science to IX Standard students. The results of the study revealed that experiment group performed better than the control group due to the exposure of multimedia based learning. Thus multimedia helps the students to sustain their interest and also their retention power compared to the traditional method of teaching. The constant use of multimedia will make students understand more and achieve more in their academic achievement. Hence it was concluded that the multimedia approach is considered to be one of the best techniques for biology teaching at IX standard level.

Ponraj and Sivakumar (2010) studied the effectiveness of Computer-Assisted Instruction in Teaching Zoology in Relation to Learners' Personality. The major findings of the study indicated that achievement scores of experimental group students were higher than the control group students after the treatment.

Yusuf, Mudasiru and Afolabi, Adedeji (2010) investigated the effects of computer assisted instruction (CAI) on secondary school students' performance in biology. The findings of the study showed that the performance of students exposed to CAI either individually or cooperatively were better than their counterparts exposed to the conventional classroom instruction. Based on the research findings recommendations were made on the need to develop relevant CAI packages for teaching biology in Nigerian secondary schools.

OBJECTIVES

1. To know the edu-digital skill among higher secondary students in Coimbatore district.
2. To find out the effectiveness of Multimedia Programme in teaching among higher secondary students.

METHODOLOGY

Research may be termed as a systemic inquiry of verified knowledge; it is an organized deliberate effort to collect information, to analyze it, to put it together and finally to evaluate it. This research paper on methodology describes elaborately, the sample that was chosen, research design, objectives of the study, data collection, statistical techniques used for data and analysis.

Population

Population selected for this study was 100 higher secondary students in a selected school at Coimbatore District.

Attitude Scale towards Multimedia Programme

The attitude scale was used to measure the level of attitude towards Multimedia programme. The scale was constructed and validated by the investigator.

The attitude scale towards multimedia programme, consisting of 40 items, was designed by the investigator and was given to experienced teachers who were handling Computer Science in higher secondary schools, professors of Computer Science and Education and Educational psychologists. On the basis of the suggestions of above experts, some items were restructured and some were eliminated. Finally 25 items were selected for this test. The scale for measuring the higher secondary student's attitude towards multimedia programme in the study is of the Likert type. This scale has as many as 25 statements of which 20 are favourable towards multimedia programme and the remaining are unfavourable towards it.

Scoring

In the Likert type of scale, against each statement, five alternatives namely "Strongly agree", "Agree", "Undecided", "Disagree", and "Strongly disagree" are given. The subjects have to indicate their choice by putting a tick-mark (√) under one of the five columns against each statement.

For favourable statement weightage of 4,3,2,1 and 0 were given from strongly agree to strongly disagree in that order. For unfavourable statements the scoring was reversed. Thus the strongly agree response will get 0 and the strongly disagree response will get 4. Here the weightage of 0,1,2,3 and 4 were given from strongly agree to the strongly disagree in that order.

Thus the score value lies between 0-100. The content validity of the tool was established based on the opinion given by the experts. The reliability of the tool was established by Split-Half method. It was found to be 0.83 which was significant.

Data Collection

Primary data, required for the present research work were collected by conducting direct interviews using questionnaire. All the respondents were given sufficient information about the Project work. These respondents were provided with the same questionnaires. They were also informed that they have to answer in the same fashion.

HYPOTHESIS

There is no significant difference between the pre and post test mean scores of experimental group students in their attitude towards multimedia programme.

Administration of retention test

The Attitude Scale towards Multimedia Programme was constructed and validated by the investigator and was administered to the subjects of the experimental group. The pre test scores on attitude towards multimedia programme were collected. Thus pre test and post test scores on attitude towards multimedia programme were computed for analysis.

ANALYSIS AND INTERPRETATION

To find out the significance of the difference between the pre and post test mean scores of experimental group students in their attitude towards multimedia programme the 't' test was used.

TABLE. 11.1: Distribution of 't' Value between the Pre and Post Test mean Scores of Experimental Group Students in their Attitude towards Multimedia Programme

Group	N	Mean	S.D	't' value	Level of Significant
Pre test	50	42.08	10.42	24.47	$p<0.05$
Post test	50	93.58	2.57		

There is no significant difference between the pre and post test mean scores of experimental group students in their attitude towards multimedia programme.

The obtained 't' value is statistically significant since it is greater than the table 't' value 1.96 at 0.05 level of significance. Hence the null hypothesis is rejected. It shows that there is significant difference between the pre and post test mean scores of experimental group students in their attitude towards multimedia programme. It is therefore concluded that the experimental group students show more favourable attitude towards multimedia programme in the post test than the pre test.

TABLE. 11.2: Showing the Stepwise Regression Analysis Predicting Factors Influencing Effectiveness of Edu-digital Skill among Higher Secondary Students and Demographic Variables

Sl. No	Step/Source	Unstandardized Coefficients Beta	Std. Error	Standardized Coefficients Beta Beta	Step t	P
1.	Gender	1.144	0.156	0.242	7.324	0.01
2.	Father education	1.254	0.359	0.163	3.495	0.01
3.	Mother education	2.615	0.462	0.361	5.661	0.01
4.	Monthly Income	2.175	0.402	0.280	5.410	0.01
5.	Father Occupation	1.022	0.513	0.137	1.992	0.01

* P < 0.01

Five variables viz Gender, Father education, Mother education, Monthly income and Father Occupation have significantly contributed for predicting the factors influencing effectiveness of edu-digital skill among higher secondary. The first variable Gender seems to be 7.324, Father education seems to be 3.495, Mother education seems to be 5.661, Monthly income seems to be 5.410 and Father occupation seems to be 1.992. The predictive value of these variables separately is 0.01.

TABLE. 11.3: Showing the Correlation between the Effectiveness of Edu-Digital Skill among Higher Secondary Students and Demographic Variables

Factors	Effectiveness of edu-digital skill among higher secondary students
Gender	0.920**
Father education	0.849**
Mother education	0.914**
Monthly Income	0.880**
Father Occupation	0.855**

* Significant at 0.01 level

Effectiveness of edu-digital skill among higher secondary students is positively and significantly related to Gender (0.920), Father education (0.849), Mother education (0.914), Monthly income (0.880) and Father occupation (0.855). So, the direct relationship between the effectiveness of edu-digital skill among higher secondary students and selected demographic variables.

Conclusion

Computer and multimedia technology for education offers a number of benefits. They allow the teacher to structure and present the information with varying special effects to the students. They can also be used for the storage of audio-visual information of various types. Multimedia programmes provide a lot of benefits. The benefits for learners include flexibility of scheduled instruction at a location convenient to learners, reduced student time, assured progress in skill development, increased achievement and increased retention and continuous report to the learners of progress and accomplishments, specified performance criteria, good response and feedback.

The application of multimedia programme would definitely create a good learning environment in classroom, sustaining attention and motivating the students to learn effectively. The application of multimedia may create a congenial learning climate in schools and can bring real life situations.

The investigator has chosen the topic for the present study in order to address the problem faced by teachers, teaching science, to foster involvement in new teaching approaches, to get a feeling of satisfaction through learning in the classroom, to create joyful learning environment and to stimulate active information processing for effective learning,

In a vast country like India, enormous work is now being done in the field of education, but it is still not possible to equip each and every school with all the facilities for teaching science. Secondary schools need high quality teaching aids. Multimedia, as a teaching aid, is very much effective with colour, sound and graphics, which are found in the audio, video movie media. Any diagram can be explained in detail with 3D effects, which helps the students understand clearly. The students can get a live vision of life's aspects and scientific factors. Multimedia includes use of computer.

The present study has found out that the multimedia programme is very effective in higher secondary level. As the present teaching-learning process in higher secondary classes is very rigid, time bound and outmoded, it was proposed to use multimedia programme.

As multimedia programme develops a favourable attitude towards multimedia programme, motivates the students to involve in the process of learning, attracts students' attention in learning, accelerates the students' understanding of concepts of subjects, increases the retention power and that it is highly suitable for all categories of students ranging from low to high achievers, it is suggested that this multimedia programme be widely adopted and implemented in educational institutions as computer laboratory facilities are available in all the schools and colleges to enable the learners to learn the subjects of their choice according to their own pace and ability. Learning through multimedia programme is very easy, understandable and comfortable to all categories of students for all types of subjects. ❐

12

Awareness of Flip Teaching among School Teachers

"A Quality education has the power to transform societies in a single generation, provide children with the protection they need from the hazards of poverty, labor exploitation and disease and give them the knowledge, skills and confidence to reach their full potential". India needs multi-dimensional and broad based quality education to maintain its leader ship in the 21st century. Therefore India should show the concern over the quality in education as the education in India is not competitive in terms of the quality with other countries. The FLIP classroom is the latest learning model to have taken the teaching and training world by storm.

In a flipped classroom content normally delivered in lectures is covered by students in their own time, often through the use of video or readings. Face-to-face time is used for activities where the focus is on learning through experience. It allows teachers and trainers to flip through concepts, which in turn gives them more time to interact with students instead of lecturing. This is also known as backwards classroom, reverse instruction, flipping the classroom and reverse teaching. The flip classroom is ideal for adult education and training, where students are more self-motivated and focused. This model of learning compliments training objectives which are 'actionable' rather than passive objectives like 'awareness or comprehension'.

Significance of the Study

This study is undertaken to find out the awareness of flip teaching among school teachers in and around Madurai District. This study gave them the clear knowledge about Flip teaching is a form of blended learning in which students learn new content online by watching video lectures, usually at home, and what used to be homework (assigned problems) is now done in class with teachers offering more personalized guidance and interaction with students, instead of lecturing. This is also known as backwards classroom, flipped classroom, reverse teaching, and the Thayer Method

Background of the Study

This study was done in and around Madurai city. The need of today is quality of education. If the quality is maintained in all the above we can produce professionally skillful students who are going to the meet the future global citizens. So it is necessary to have innovative teaching methods or alternative methods in imparting knowledge among the students. The traditional pattern of teaching has been to assign students to read textbooks and work on problem sets outside school, while listening to lectures and taking tests in class.

Traditionally, the teacher engages with the students who ask questions — but those who don't ask tend to need the most attention. "We refer to 'silent failures, " said one teacher, claiming that flipping allows her to target those who need the most help rather than the most confident. Flipping changes teachers from "sage on the stage" to "guide on the side", allowing them to work with individuals or groups of students throughout the session. The Investigator wanted to know whether there is awareness of flip teaching among school teachers in and around Madurai District

Objectives of the Study

1. To measure and find out whether there is awareness of flip teaching among school teachers in and around Madurai District
2. To enable the teachers to sensitize the today's needed to turn towards the flip teaching and classrooms.

Hypotheses

1. Awareness of flip teaching among school teachers in and around Madurai District are high
2. There is significant difference in the awareness of flip teaching among school teachers with regard to the board of institution. [Matriculation and CBSE]
3. There is significant difference in the awareness of flip teaching among school teachers with regard to the gender. [Male & Female]

Methodology Used

The survey method was taken and target population is the school teachers who are teaching in various boards such as Matriculation and CBSE in and around Madurai district. The size of the samples of the present study is 60 teachers.

Tool Construction

The self made check list was used to find out whether there is awareness of flip teaching among school teachers in and around Madurai District. The checklist had 20 items

Administration of the Tool

The photocopies of the check-list were distributed to the teachers of four educational institutions in and around Madurai. The filled in questionnaires were corrected analyzed and interpreted.

Statistical Technique Used

Calculating mean value,'t' test

Table Shows the Number of Teachers from Four Schools

S.No.	Name of the school	Institution	Total no	F	M
1	S.S.V.Sala	Matriculation	15	15	-
2	Le Chatlier	Matriculation	15		15
3	PVK Academy	CBSE	15	8	7
4	Vellammal	CBSE	15	7	8
		Total	**60**	**30**	**30**

Hypothesis: 1

Awareness of flip teaching among school teachers in and around Madurai District are high

TABLE. 12.2: Showing the Mean Value

Name of the School	Total	Sex		Board	Over All Mean
		Female	Male		
S.S.V.Sala	15	15	-	Matriculation	7.5
Le Chatlier	15		15	Matriculation	9
PVK Academy	15	8	7	CBSE	8.5
Vellammal	15	7	8	CBSE	9.5

It is inferred from the above table that there is no Awareness of flip teaching among school teachers in and around Madurai District. All the mean scores indicated that they are less than the theoretical mean (10). Still there were no innovative teaching methods were followed to reach the global standard as well as to improve the low achievers.

Hypothesis: 2

There is significant difference in the awareness of flip teaching among school teachers with regard to the board of institution. [Matriculation and CBSE]

TABLE. 12.3: Showing the Difference between the Variables

S.No	Variable	Mean	Std. dev	't'	Significance at 0.5 level
1	Matriculation	8.25	0.50	0.93	No Significant
2	CBSE	9	0.74		

It is inferred from the above table that the't' value is 0.93 is lesser than the't' value 1.96 at 0.5 level of significance. So the research hypothesis is rejected. The result indicated that there is no significant difference in the awareness of flip teaching among school teachers with regard to the board of institution. [Matriculation and CBSE]

Hypothesis: 3

There is significant difference in the awareness of flip teaching among school teachers with regard to the gender. [Male & Female]

TABLE.12.4: Showing the Difference between the Variables

S.No	Variable	mean	Std.dev	't'	Significance at 0.5 level
1	Female	8.5	1.25	0.98	No Significant
2	male	9	0.57		

It is inferred from the above table that the't' value is 0.98 is lesser than the't' value 1.96 at 0.5 level of significance. So the research hypothesis is rejected. The result indicated that there is no significant difference in the awareness of flip teaching among school teachers with regard to the gender. [Male & Female]

Hypotheses Verification

There is significant difference in the awareness of flip teaching among school teachers with regard to the board of institution. [Matriculation and CBSE] is rejected. There is significant difference in the awareness of flip teaching among school teachers with regard to the gender. [Male & Female] is rejected.

Delimitation

The samples are taken from only from four schools in and around Madurai area and also restricted to the variable that is type of institution and gender alone. In this study the Investigator use only mean and't' test as the statistical treatment .This was also delimitation.

Scope of the Study

This study can highlight the need for the alternative, creative, student friendly, user friendly and innovative methods of teaching. The flip classroom is the latest learning model to have taken the teaching and training world by storm. The flip teaching models are being incorporated by teachers of all subjects, for students of all ages. This mode of learning is now slowly making inroads into the teaching and training in India. The flip classroom is ideal for adult education and training, where students are more self-motivated and focused. This model of learning compliments training objectives which are 'actionable' rather than passive objectives like 'awareness or comprehension'.

Suggestion for the Future

1. We can take more schools for the study
2. We can take so many variables
3. We can also use extend all the boards of schools in future.

Educational Implications

This Study revealed that there is a need for considering another scenario where in students has already gone through a video lecture on the second conditional at their own time. They can rewind, pause and repeat the lecture as many times as they want. Additionally, they do graded exercises to practice the concept and take up an assessment to check their proficiency. Both the learner and the facilitator now know what to focus on and the class is much more productive for the learner. The facilitator only has to provide solutions for problem areas. Flip training can help overcome the constraints and make learning a focused and productive experience for the learner.

❐

13

Tremendous Revolution in Education

There is a tremendous revolution in science and technology. Information in communication technologies has a deep Cultural Revolution changing. There is a need to make a realistic assessment of what technology cannot do to reach a plateau of productivity when the technology consistently delivers to realistic goals.

The Impact of Science and Technology among Students

Digital skill is a vast technique used by all people. Educational technology and mobile learning, multi- media learning are all digital skill. Science is a boon. Man has discovered many wonderful things from the treasure of developing every day. It has made our life easier, happier and more secure. Science and technology has conquered time and space. It has made very good communication and made the transport easier. With the help of science and technology, modern medicine and medical treatments, the doctors save the life of sick people from the jaws of death. Many organs are now transplanted. It is used in the field of agriculture. The impact of science and technology among students in the field is both good and bad.

Science laboratory, space centre ISRO are taken in the highest form. Television, telecommunication, type- recorder, films, LCD projectors, digital and white board, e- learning, e-teaching, teleconferencing, teaching machine cell phones such as all types of multimedia are boons to us. But the students are affected by this because of misusing. So they blamed science. We cannot blame science; it is a wonderful boon.

Digital Skill in Website

By the wrong use of face book, web site, web-camera, especially cell phones, net connection, lab top etc. Science and technology become down. But once for all where we use science and technology in proper, correct and perfect way it is a boon to us otherwise it is curse and demon to us. A secondary Information and Communication Technology curriculum should contribute to the building up of teams of professionals with these new competencies. The use of Information and Communication Technology cuts across all aspects of economic and social life. Technological developments in Information and Communication Technology are very rapid. Technology quickly becomes obsolete requiring new skills and knowledge to be mastered frequently. Adaptation is only possible when based on a sound understanding of the principles and concepts of Information and Communication Technology.

REVIEW OF LITERATURE

Lei, Jing (2010) studied on Quantity versus Quality: A New Approach to Examine the Relationship between Technology Use and Student Outcomes. It is found that that to examine the relationship between technology use and student outcomes, the quality of technology use-how, and what, technology is used--is a more significant factor than the quantity of technology use--how much technology is used. This argument was exemplified by an empirical study that used both angles to examine the association between technology use and student outcomes. When only the quantity of technology use was examined, no significant association was observed. However, when the quality of technology was examined by investigating the specific types of technology uses, a significant association was identified between technology use and all student outcomes. Furthermore, different types of technology use showed different influences on specific student outcomes. General technology uses were positively associated with student technology proficiency, while subject-specific technology uses were negatively associated with student technology proficiency. Social-communication technology uses were significantly positively associated with developmental outcomes such as self-esteem and positive attitude towards school. Entertainment/exploration technology use showed significant positive association with student learning habits. None of these technology uses had significant influence on student academic outcome.

Chen, Rong-Ji (2010) studied on Investigating Models for Preserves Teachers' Use of Technology to Support Student-Centered Learning. The study addressed two limitations of previous research on factors related to teachers' integration of technology in their teaching. It attempted to test a structural equation model (SEM) of the relationships among a set of variables influencing preserves teachers' use of technology specifically to support student-centered learning. A review of literature led to a path model that provided the design and analysis for the study, which involved 206, preserves teachers in the United States. The results show that the proposed model had a moderate fit to the observed data, and a more parsimonious model was found to have a better fit. In addition, preserves teachers' self-efficacy of teaching with technology had the strongest influence on technology use, which was mediated by their perceived value of teaching and learning with technology. School's contextual factors had moderate influence on technology use. Moreover, the effect of preserves teachers' training on student-centered technology use was mediated by both perceived value and self-efficacy of technology. The implications for teacher preparation include close collaboration between teacher education program and field experience, focusing on specific technology uses.

Eisenberg, Mike; Johnson, Doug; Berkowitz, Bob (2010) studied on Information, Communications, and Technology (ICT) Skills Curriculum Based on the Big6 Skills Approach to Information Problem-Solving. There is clear and widespread agreement among the public and educators that all students need to be proficient technology users. Technology literacy is among the attributes that appear in nearly every set of "21st Century Skills." However, while districts spend a great deal of money on technology, there seems to be only a vague notion of what technology literacy really means. Defining and describing technology skills is only a first step to assure all children become proficient information and technology users. Other critical elements will include a teacher-supported scope and sequence of skills, well designed projects, and effective assessments. Equally essential is fruitful collaboration among classroom teachers, teacher librarians, and technology teachers in order to present students with a unified and integrated approach to ensure that all children master the skills they will need to thrive in an information-rich future. This article presents the "Information, Communications, and Technology (ICT) Skills for Information Problem Solving" curriculum which defines technology capabilities and identifies associated skills based on the Big6 Skills Approach. The Curriculum describes levels of technology proficiency, and in so doing, promotes the skills and concepts basic to information and technology. In an information society, it is essential that students are technologically productive and able to solve information problems effectively and efficiently. This curriculum requires more than teaching computer skills, technology hardware, and software programs in an isolated approach. An effective technology curriculum must be integrated across content areas and grade levels to improve the learning process. Technology is successfully integrated when it seamlessly supports curricular goals. Students learn and refine their technology skills when they work on projects that require them to solve problems and make decisions.

Savage, Robert S.; Erten, Ozlem; Abrami, Philip; Hipps, Geoffrey; Comaskey, Erin; van Lierop, Dea (2010) studied on ABRACADABRA in the Hands of Teachers: The Effectiveness of a Web-Based Literacy Intervention in Grade 1 Language Arts Programs . Each teacher chose to use the program in qualitatively distinct ways that corresponded to the first three stages of Sandholtz, Ringstaff, and Dwyer's (1997) technology integration model, namely: "Entry," "Adoption" and "Adaptation." Growth in literacy between pre- and post-test revealed significant differences associated with technology integration style across all measures of literacy and related language skills. The largest and most-widespread effects were evident for the "Adaptation" group that linked technology content to wider learning themes in the classroom. In terms of overall growth in standardised literacy scores across all six such measures used, Adaptation proved to be 60% more effective than Adoption. Results suggest that explorations of exactly how teachers use technology have important implications for practice as well as for the interpretation of field-based studies of the effectiveness of educational technology.

Jun, Han; Zhuzhu, Wang (2010) studied on Capability Building in Educational Technology for Teachers in China. This paper gives a brief introduction to the project called Education Technology Capacity Building Plan for All Primary and Secondary Teachers now being implemented in China. Because information and communication technology skills training cannot match the demand of teachers' professional development, the Chinese Ministry of Education established the education technology standard for teachers and launched the project. This paper introduced the features of standard training and testing, and discusses the output and influence of the project.

McGarr, Oliver (2010) studied on Education for Sustainable Development in Technology Education in Irish Schools: A Curriculum Analysis. This paper explores the integration of Education for Sustainable Development (ESD) in technology education and the extent to which it is currently addressed in curriculum documents and state examinations in technology education at post-primary level in Ireland. This analysis is conducted amidst the backdrop of considerable change in technology education at post-primary level. The analysis of the provision of technology education found, that among the range of technology related subjects offered, the study of Technology and Society is only addressed in one in a comprehensive manner. The paper discusses the implications of this limited integration, examines the factors inhibiting greater integration of ESD and outlines opportunities for future development.

Waring, Scott M. (2010) studied on The Impact of a Technology Coordinator's Belief System upon Using Technology to Create a Community's History. As it has been shown that teachers of social studies content are less likely than teachers of other content areas to utilize technology in their classroom, this study focuses on one instructional technology coordinators' beliefs towards technology, instruction, and students and how these beliefs impacted how technology was utilized during a technology-enriched community history project with a group of fourth-grade students. It was determined that the instructional technology coordinators' beliefs included the following: (a) technology should serve as a tool and should be seamlessly integrated into the curriculum; (b) the teacher should construct meaningful experiences that allow students to become engaged in the learning process; however, before guiding student discovery, the teacher needs to explicitly teach basic technological skills; (c) and all students are able to learn and are capable of engaging in independent problem solving and critical thinking at some level. Her beliefs manifested themselves daily, particularly in the way that she approached instruction and integrated technology seamlessly into the curriculum. Through this study, it was found that the technology coordinator's beliefs toward technology, instruction, and her students directly impacted how technology was used in her classroom.

Jun, Han; Zhuzhu, Wang (2010) studied on Capability Building in Educational Technology for Teachers in China. This paper gives a brief introduction to the project called Education Technology Capacity Building Plan for All Primary and Secondary Teachers now being implemented in China. Because information and communication technology skills training cannot match the demand of teachers' professional development, the Chinese Ministry of Education established the education technology standard for teachers and launched the project. This paper introduced the features of standard training and testing, and discusses the output and influence of the project.

Ruzic-Dimitrijevic, Ljiljana; Dimitrijevic, Maja (2010) studied on Challenges IT Instructors Face in the Self-Education Process. We find that the earlier the instructors graduated, the smaller is the chance they studied the technologies similar to the ones they teach. We found that none of the surveyed instructors who graduated before 1979 teach a technology they studied. The analysis of the survey also supports the second hypothesis. The results show that 70% of the IT instructors have to change the course syllabus every 2-3 years due to the technology changes. We also found that the majority of the instructors primarily use textbooks and online tutorials to self teach new technologies, which support the third hypothesis. By comparison, they take courses given by others and work on real life projects far less often. In contrast, most instructors agree that taking courses and working on projects would greatly help them in their self-education. Most instructors (16 out of 20) assert that the lack of time stops them from doing so, which according to the survey is found to be one of the major challenges they face in the process of self-education, supporting the fourth hypothesis. Considering the results of our research, as well as our own experience, we have identified a list of activities that make the process of self-education more efficient and/or effective for IT instructors. These activities include taking on-line tutorials, creating software programs using the environment/ language/tools covered in the courses, working on real life projects, taking organized courses, attending IT/CS conferences, seminars, and workshops, collecting experience from industry people, and using the help of advanced students. However, in order to create the time for IT instructors to apply the self-learning methods and stay on top of the new technologies, we conclude that it may be necessary that the university policy include the time for self-learning as a significant part of IT instructors' everyday duties, i.e., as a part of their "job description".

Larson, Lotta; Kuhn, Cyndi Danner; Collins, Royce Ann; Balthazor, Gerri; Ribble, Mike; Miller, Teresa Northern (2009) studied on Technology Instruction: Fixing the Disconnect. High school students spend much of their educational journeys immersed in "old" literacies of paper, pencil, and print books. But outside of the classroom, they are exposed to information and communication technologies--such as blogs, wikis, Internet browsers, multimedia, social networking sites, and a wide range of software--each of which demand new literacies. This disconnect is a serious problem for schools because it reflects a decline in school's relevancy to students' futures, and the gap between how schools teach and how students learn will only grow over time. The first step in updating a school's technology and instruction is to revisit and revise current vision statements by facilitating conversations with all stakeholders about expectations for student skills upon graduation. Vision setting must include the new literacies. Teachers and education leaders must model expectations and support visionary teaching and learning through technology. To make that happen, they need instructional technology specialists who not only have a strong knowledge of hardware, networks, and equipment maintenance but also understand the art of teaching and how to enhance and enrich the daily curriculum by integrating technology. To do this, instructional technology staff members and those creating the curriculum must engage in ongoing dialogue to ensure that computer language is translated into the language of teaching and is directly related to what teachers want to do in their classrooms. For schools to successfully integrate technology, leaders must encourage and support strong relationships between teachers and technology support staff members. Schools must also provide easy access to technology in classrooms so that teachers can effectively integrate technology into the curriculum. Limited resources and complicated check-out procedures often contribute to lack of use. In addition, frustrations over blocked sites or limited access to online resources prevent teachers from integrating technology. Leaders, teachers, and technology staff members need ongoing communication with one another to share needs, frustrations, and solutions. Schools must move ahead quickly. It may be understandable for teachers and leaders to be a bit behind in the use of technology, but it is no longer adequate or appropriate to hold students back. Students today will be leaders in a global society, and technology can connect them to that world in ways that were unimaginable 10 years ago. School leaders need to join students in their world--which includes all of the new literacies--so that everyone can function and contribute to the future.

OBJECTIVES

1. To study the level of teachers attitude towards using new technology in teaching
2. To find out whether there is any significant relationship between teachers attitude towards the use of new technology and their interest in teaching.

METHODOLOGY

The methodology adopted for the study is explained in detail. The sampling technique, size of the sample, variables of the study, description of the tool used and administration of tool are elaborated.

Sample

The study was conducted on 100 school teachers, Coimbatore district, Tamil Nadu.

Data Collection

Primary data, required for the present research work were collected by conducting direct interviews using questionnaire. All the respondents were given sufficient information about the study. These respondents were provided with the same questionnaires. They were also informed that they have to answer in the same fashion.

ANALYSIS AND INTERPRETATION

Gender and attitude towards the use of new technology

Null Hypothesis No. 1.

There is no significant difference between male and female teachers attitude towards the use of new technology.

TABLE. 13.1: The Significance of the Difference ('t' value) between mean Scores of Male and Female Teacher's Attitude Towards the use of New Technology

Gender	N	Mean	SD	't' value	Level of Significance (0.05)
Male	50	100.30	11.81	4.89	Significant
Female	50	107.30	12.57		

It is evident from the table the calculated 't' value is 4.89 is significant at 0.05 level. Hence, the framed null hypothesis is rejected and research hypothesis is accepted. It is inferred that there is significant difference found between male and female teachers attitude towards the use of new technology.

Qualification and Attitude Towards the use of New Technology

Null Hypothesis No. 2

There is no significant difference between undergraduate and post graduate teachers with respect to their attitude towards the use of new technology.

TABLE. 13.2: The Significance of the Difference ('t' value) between Undergraduate and Post Graduate Teachers with Respect to their Attitude Towards the use of New Technology.

Qualification	N	Mean	SD	't' value	Level of Significance (0.05)
Under graduate	35	103.64	11.44	0.28	Not Significant
Post graduate	65	103.23	13.53		

It is evident from the table the calculated 't' value is 0.28 which is not significant at 0.05 level. Hence, the framed null hypothesis is accepted. It shows that there is no significant difference between undergraduate and post graduate teachers with respect to their attitude towards the use of new technology.

Locality of the School and Attitude towards the use of New Technology

Null Hypothesis No. 3

There is no significant difference between rural and urban school teachers attitude towards the use of new technology.

TABLE. 13.3: The Significance of the Difference ('t' value) between Rural and Urban School Teachers Attitude Towards the use of New Technology

Locality of the school	N	Mean	SD	't' value	Level of Significance (0.05)
Rural	65	103.42	11.23	0.06	Not Significant
Urban	35	103.33	14.15		

It is evident from the table the calculated 't' value is 0.06 which is not significant at 0.05 level. Hence, the framed null hypothesis is accepted. It shows that there is no significant difference between rural and urban school teachers attitude towards the use of new technology.

Type of School and Attitude towards the use of New Technology

Null Hypothesis No. 4

There is no significant difference between private and government school teachers attitude towards the use of new technology.

TABLE. 13.4: The Significance of the Difference ('t' value) between Private and Government School Teachers Attitude Towards the use of New Technology

Type of School	N	Mean	SD	't' value	Level of Significance (0.05)
Private	65	104.79	11.54	1.26	Not Significant
Government	35	102.78	13.01		

It is evident from the table the calculated 't' value is 1.26 which is not significant at 0.05 level. Hence, the framed null hypothesis is accepted. It shows that there is no significant difference between private and government school teachers attitude towards the use of new technology.

Level of Teaching and Attitude towards the use of New Technology

Null Hypothesis No. 5

There is no significant difference between secondary and higher secondary school teachers attitude towards the use of new technology.

TABLE. 13.5: The Significance of the Difference ('t' test) between Secondary and Higher Secondary School Teachers Attitude Towards the use of New Technology

Level of Teaching	N	Mean	SD	't' value	Level of Significance (0.05)
Secondary School	60	102.12	12.12	1.85	Not Significant
Higher secondary School	40	104.82	13.03		

It is evident from the table the calculated 't' value is 1.85 which is not significant at 0.05 level. Hence, the framed null hypothesis is accepted. It is inferred that there is no significant difference between secondary and higher secondary school teachers attitude towards the use of new technology.

Teaching Experience and Attitude Towards the use of New Technology

Null Hypothesis No. 6

There is no significant difference among teachers who have different years of teaching experience with respect to their attitude towards the use of new technology.

TABLE. 13.6: The Significance of the difference ('F' test) among School Teachers with Respect to their Attitude Towards the use of New Technology

Teaching Experience	Sum of Squares	Mean Squares	df	'F' Value	Level of Significance (0.05)
Between Groups	2281.690	1140.845	2	7.48	Significant
Within Groups	45273.227	152.435	97		
Total	**47554.917**	-	**99**		

It is evident from the table the calculated 'F' value is 7.48 which is significant at 0.05 level. Hence, the framed null hypothesis is rejected and research hypothesis is accepted. It is inferred that there is significant difference among teachers who have different years of teaching experience with respect to their attitude towards the use of new technology.

TABLE. 13.7: The Significance of the Difference ('t' test) between Teachers who have Different Years of Teaching Experience with Respect to their Attitude Towards the use of New Technology

Teaching experience	N	Mean	SD	't' value	Level of Significance (0.05)
Below 10 years	49	109.33	11.05	3.06	Significant
10-20 years	20	103.03	12.80		
Above 20 years	31	101.67	12.47	4.16	Significant
Below 10 years	49	109.33	11.05		
10-20 years	20	103.03	12.80	0.81	Not Significant
Above 20 years	31	101.67	12.47		

From table, it is revealed that there is significant difference between teachers who have below 10 years of teaching experience and 10-20 years of teaching experience and teachers who have above 20 years of teaching experience and below 10 years of teaching experience. Whereas no significant difference is found between teachers who have above 20 years of teaching experience and 10-20 years of teaching experience.

CORRELATION ANALYSIS

Correlation Analysis between Teachers Attitude Towards the use of New Technology and Interest in Teaching

One of the important objectives of the present investigation is to study the significant relationship between teacher's attitude towards the use of new technology and interest in teaching. For this purpose, the investigator applied the co-efficient of correlation ('r'). The computed values are given in the table. The investigator also framed a null hypothesis for testing the relationship between teacher's attitude towards the use of new technology and interest in teaching.

Null hypothesis No. 8

There is no significant relationship between teacher's attitude towards the use of new technology and interest in teaching.

TABLE. 13.8: Co-Efficient of Correlation betweenTteacher's Attitude Towards the use of New Technology and Interest in Teaching

Correlation	N	'r' value	Level of Significance at 0.05 level
Teacher's attitude towards the use of new technology and interest in teaching	100	0.56	Significant

It is evident from the table the computed correlation coefficient 'r' for entire sample is 0.56, which is significant at 0.05 level. Hence, the framed null hypothesis is rejected. It is inferred that there is significant relationship found between teacher's attitude towards the use of new technology and their interest in teaching.

SUGGESTIONS

The present study gives a clear-cut view about the present position of teachers attitude towards the use of new technology and their interest in teaching. Based on the important findings stated earlier the following recommendations are suggested.

1. Teachers must be provided with adequate opportunities to enhance their knowledge in new technologies and equipments. The government should provide more effective environment through schools for them to improve their skills in application of new technologies in teaching.
2. Periodical in-service training programmes should be organized to keep their interest and quest in teaching.

3. The finding of the present study reveals that the teachers have neutral attitude towards the use of new technology in teaching and low interest in teaching. This indicates that the Heads of the institutions must look into the varied problems that influence the interest of teachers and find amicable solutions to their difficulties.
4. More activities should be planned in the curriculum to bring forth different modes of creative expressions which will provide competition and generate interest of teachers in teaching.
5. Sincere work and involved performances of teachers must be recognized and honoured by the authorities. And application of innovative methods and technologies in instruction must be encouraged.
6. In addition with the above recommendation the government and all the other concerned authorities should realize the problems of experienced teachers and provide conductive environment of growth and mutual help of teachers should be ensured.

Conclusion

The present study is conducted on teachers attitude towards the use of new technologies in teaching and their interest in teaching. The findings of the present study revealed that the teachers have neutral attitude towards the use of new technology and low interest in teaching. Therefore, the authorities and government should find suitable measures to improve the interest of teachers in teaching and the application of innovative technologies in Teaching Learning Process.

❒

14

Learning Styles of Higher Secondary Students in Biological Science in Villupuram D.

As teachers, our goal is to encourage learning in our classrooms. But what is learning, and what principles or factors affect how our students learn? In this section, we provide you with the very basics of what learning is, how and when it occurs, and how to structure your lessons to maximize student learning.

There are three components to the definition of Learning:

1. **"Learning is a process, not a product."** Exam scores and term papers are measures of learning, but they are not the process of learning itself.
2. **"Learning is a change in knowledge, beliefs, behaviors or attitudes."** This change requires time, particularly when one is dealing with changes to core beliefs, behaviors, and attitudes. Don't interpret a lack of sea change in your students' beliefs or attitudes immediately following a lesson as a lack of learning on their part, but instead, consider that such a change will take time – perhaps a few weeks, perhaps until the end of the term, or even longer.
3. **"Learning is not something done to students, but something that students themselves do."** If ycu have ever carefully planned a lesson, only to find that your students just didn't "get it," consider that your lesson should be designed not just to impart knowledge but also to lead students through the process of their own learning.

Learning is the process by which one acquires, ingests, and stores or accepts information. Our experiences with learned information compose our bodies of knowledge. Learning is a process unique to each individual. Some learn quickly, scanning the information and mastering the concept or skill seemingly effortlessly. Others stumble while processing information, taking longer to grasp the concept or requiring numerous exposures over a sustained period of time. Some individuals store the information they've learned indefinitely, cementing it in their memories. Others find that the information they've learned slips away rapidly. Some learn best through text, others through practice, some through hearing. Learning styles are as unique and varied as our personalities. Learning is a lifelong endeavor. As long as one remains engaged in life, learning does not cease. Until recently most people took learning styles for granted and left them to instinct. Realization that studying how learning should come before everything else is spreading in the world of education skill in this field can multiply efficiency.

The use of higher level work skills can bring improvement in almost all fields. Improvement in athletic field and industrial productivity has been achieved in the way. Everyone is familiar with the difference in output of a self-taught typist who uses one finger of each hand and an expert who was taught the tough system. Other experiments has shown that the level of performance on such tasks as card sorting, pitch discrimination and puzzle solving is affected by the method employed and the limit to performance might be improved of better work was used.

These findings on effects of work methods on levels of performance led to the significant theoretical contribution to theories regarding the causes of individual difference in competence. It was long assumed that these differences were primarily due to two factors. (1) Learning and (2) Amount of training in a task. Dr. Seashare after studying may findings on effects of work method, concluded that method of work was a third variable in instruction. It is found that new levels in achievement are possible by improving the learning styles.

Both in common speech and educational literature the word "Read" is used to designate a wide variety of learned activities from the socially undesirable to the highly ethnical, form bodily skill, such as walking to mental activities such as learning of critical thinking and from specified abilities to generalized attitudes. The meaning of learning includes the ideal of facility in the performance of an act, combined with a persisting inclination towards the repetition of the act.

As Bagley has said "To teach a child to study effectively is to do that most valuable thing that could be done to help him adjust himself to any environment of modern civilized life into which they live.

In 1917 strays and Newsworthy declared "Many teachers have taught subjects, but not how to study subjects, the latter is more important". H.R. Bhatia says, "unless opportunities for doing and respecting things are afforded to children it is futile to expect them to form habits". Sevmors and exhortations may help children to acquire normal vocabulary but not normal character. Percepta in the formation of learning unless children are afforded actual practice in those modes behaviour.

REVIEW OF LITERATURE

Mary Lou Koran, John J. Koran (2006), conducted a study "Interaction of Learner aptitudes with question packing in learning from prose, he suggested that, in some cases, reduction in certain information Processing requirements may actually be an important prerequisite to affective utilization of other aptitudes (learning).

The over-all means used in the analysis are presented, both low and high aptitude students in "favourable" classrooms had higher achievements scores than the two groups in 'unfavourable' classroom. This contexts effect was present to some extent in both third and fourth grade class room aptitude, third grade students. It appears that being in a classroom with many high-altitude students is beneficial for low-altitude students and some high-altitude students as well".

K.S Kahlon and Vinod Uppalo, (2007) studied on "women's aptitude and achievement in Relation to achievement motivation.

The Result of the present investigation fully supports the hypotheses on the basis of which the study had been undertaken.

1. There is significant, but imperfect relationship between aptitude (learning style) and academic achievement.
2. Discrepancy between aptitude (Learning style) and achievement bears no relationship with ability.
3. Discrepancy between aptitude (Learning Style) and achievement bears significant relationship with academic achievement.
4. Discrepancy between aptitude and achievement bears significant relationship with achievement motivation. That is, high achievement motivation goes with positive discrepancy where as low achievement motivation accounts for negative discrepancy"

Robert B. Burnes (2012) conducted a study on "The Relation of Aptitudes of Learning at different Points in the time during Instruction: The result of this study suggested that some aptitude-learning relations are not stable over time and that his instability is exhibited in different aptitudes being required at different points in time during instruction. These findings supported most of the Junior evidence examining aptitude correlates at different stages of learning and did not support the assumption made in ATI Research that aptitudes relate equally to learning for the during of treatment"

Moraddwaj Varma (2013) conducted a study on "Comparative achievement in science of Tharu Tribals and other at high school level. He found, that the achievement of Tharu tribals is lower than that of the non-tharus in all the three science subjects were significant at .01 level"

In Jamur (2013) made a study in Patna in relationship between study habits and achievement. His study showed a correlation of 0.51 between study habits and achievement of students and a correlation of 0.144 between study habits and intelligence.

OBJECTIVES

1. To study the higher secondary learning styles in Biological science.
2. To know the higher secondary different methods learning styles in Biological science.
3. To find out the higher secondary factors learning styles in Biological science.

METHODOLOGY

The methodology adopted for the study is explained in detail. The sampling technique, size of the sample, variables of the study, description of the tool used and administration of tool are elaborated.

Sample

The sample selected for the present study is 100 higher secondary students in Villupuram district. Random sampling technique was used for the selection of sample.

Data Collection

Primary data, required for the present research work were collected by conducting direct interviews using questionnaire. All the respondents were given sufficient information about the Project work. These respondents were provided with the same questionnaires. They were also informed that they have to answer in the same fashion.

Tools Used in the Study

SOLAT Tool of learning style D. Venketraman (1986) consists of 25 items. The learning style comprises 5 categories.

1. Verbal (1 to 5 items)
2. Content preference (6 to 10 items)

3. Class preference (11 to 15 items)
4. Learning preference (16 to 20 items)
5. Interest (20 to 25 items)

Scoring Procedure

The maximum score that a student obtains is 50 the minimum score that a student gain is 25.

Each item has two alternatives. If the student chooses the First alternative one mark is given. If the student chooses Second alternative the student it secures 2 marks. The first alternative of an item indicates the use of Right hemisphere of the brain and the second alternative of an item indicates the use of left hemisphere of the brain.

Tool Validity and Reliability

The main attributes needed to be considered regarding a good tool are validity and reliability.

Validity

A measuring instrument is said to be valid if it measures what it purpose to measure. Validity may be defined as the extent to which an instrument or a test does the job derived of it. The kind of validity and the extent or degrees to which it should be established are the major consideration while establishing validity.In the present study the researcher found out the content validity. Content validity gives the logical evidence that the content of the items of a test is suitable for the purpose for which the test is designed and used. Content validity is established is 0.549.

Reliability

The efficiency of measuring the different items are called on aspect of reliability. Reliability determined test-retest method and it is found to be validity of the tool is (0.82).

HYPOTHESIS

1. The level of learning styles among higher secondary students on the basis of their demographic variables.
2. The level of different method learning styles among higher secondary students on the basis of their demographic variables.
3. The level of factors learning styles among higher secondary students on the basis of their demographic variables.

ANALYSIS AND INTERPRETATION

TABLE. 14.1: Showing the Stepwise Regression Analysis Predicting learning Styles among Higher Secondary Students and Demographic Variables

Sl.No	Step/Source	Unstandardized Coefficients Beta	Std. Error	Standardized Coefficients Beta Beta	Step t	P
1.	Gender	1.342	0.343	1.245	5.432	0.01
2.	Locality	1.224	0.392	0.269	6.641	0.01
3.	Family Income	1.924	0.549	0.149	4.142	0.01
4.	Father Education	2.334	0.667	0.108	5.339	0.01

* P < 0.01

Four variables viz Gender, Locality, Family income and Father Education have significantly contributed for predicting the learning styles among higher secondary students. The Gender seems to be 5.432, Locality seems to be 6.641, Family income seems to be 4.142 and Father education seems to be 5.339. The predictive value of these variables separately is 0.01.

TABLE. 14.2: Showing the Stepwise Regression Analysis Predicting Different Method learning Styles and Demographic Variables

Sl.No	Step/Source	Unstandardized Coefficients Beta	Std. Error	Standardized Coefficients Beta Beta	Step t	P
1.	Type of Family	1.133	0.505	0.434	2.246	0.01
2.	Religion	1.248	0.466	0.782	2.677	0.01
3.	Community	1.792	0.683	0.646	2.625	0.01
4.	Birth Place	2.338	0.670	0.954	3.490	0.01

* P < 0.01

Four variables viz Type of family, Religion, Community and Birth place have significantly contributed for predicting the method learning styles. The first variable Type of family seems to be 2.246, Religion seems to be 2.677, Community seems to be 2.625 and Birth place seems to be 3.490. The predictive value of these variables separately is 0.01.

TABLE. 14.3: Showing the Stepwise Regression Analysis Predicting Factors learning Styles among Higher Secondary Students and Demographic Variables

Sl. No	Step/Source	Unstandardized Coefficients Beta	Std. Error	Standardized Coefficients Beta Beta	Step t	P
1.	Gender	5.195	1.030	0.824	5.041	0.01
2.	Family Monthly Income	1.809	0.451	0.443	4.016	0.01

* P < 0.01

Two variables viz Gender and Family Monthly Income have significantly contributed for predicting the factors learning styles among higher secondary. The first variable Gender seems to be 5.195, when paired with the second variable Family monthly income is 1.809. The predictive value of these variables separately is 0.01.

TABLE. 14.4: Showing the Correlation between the learning Styles of Higher Secondary Students and Demographic Variables

Factors	Learning styles of higher secondary students
Gender	0.579*
Locality	0.782**
Family Income	0.591*
Father Education	0.572*
Type of Family	0.824**

* Significant at 0.01 level ** Significant at 0.05 level

Learning styles of higher secondary students is positively and significantly related to Gender (0.579), Locality (0.782), Family Income (0.591), Father Education (0.572) and Type of family (0.824). So the direct relationship between the Learning styles of higher secondary students and demographic variables.

Conclusion

The present study aims to find out the higher secondary students learning styles. The researcher framed objectives and hypotheses on the basis of the above context. The research was carried out in 100 samples based randomly. A questionnaire constructed by R was used to collect the relevant data. After collecting the data they were analyzed using statistical tools such as Regression and Correlation analysis. The result concluded that students have average level of learning styles at Higher Secondary level in Biological science in Villupuram District.

❐

15

Awareness on Digital Tech. Applying in C.T. for Present Generation among T.Ed.

Education is the foundation stone of a Nation's intellectual power which steps its power profile. Thus, it is rightly said that it depends upon the quality of its Teachers. The destiny of India is being shaped in its classrooms. In class room Teaching, Digital Technology provides the opportunity to go beyond the class room boundaries to the outside world and events. Hence the Government is very keen in implementing the scheme of Teaching through computer in Government schools. When the Government is very much interested in the computer Teaching, It is essential that the Teachers must be well aware of the potentiality of the computer Technology. Hence the Investigators were interest to know the level of the Awareness on Digital Technology of Teacher Educators. It is a survey Research. The Investigators developed the opinion scale contains 40 statements with different dimensions such as Computer in Teaching Learning, Power point Presentation and Internet. Four points scale ranges from Strongly Agree, Agree, Strongly Disagree and Disagree was used. Developed Opinionnarie was administered to 100 Teacher Educators who are working in various Colleges of Education in Perambalur and Trichy Districts. Gender, Locality and Subject they studied were taken as the variables. The collected data was using Statistical Analysis like Mean, SD and't' test which have revealed the varied results.

Modernization is generally regarded as a process of change of traditional society into a society based on technology. As Teaching has entered the Digital age over the last several years, Technology in the Classroom is an area that all Teachers and Students are Embracing. For Teachers who have taught many years before this can be a challenging one. There are many Computer lesson plans, CDs, DVDs, audio e -books and videos available that will help in the transition. Digital Technology in the Classroom involves a lot of time and focus in its infancy, but with the Computer Lesson plans mentioned, it will develop into a fun and creative learning experience for Students and new and exciting challenges for Teachers. The incorporation of Digital technology in the education sector is important to meet the challenges presented by new trends, especially with the Global Communication of Knowledge. It is essential that the Students become familiar with the concept and use of Computer Technology in order to equip them for future job market. Similarly, the teacher can achieve better quality in Teaching Methodology.

RATIONALE OF THE STUDY

Computer plays key role in Education. Learning through Computer is an interesting affair. Now–a-days Digital Technology in Education has become the essential part of the system. In fact Teacher must well aware of the potentiality of the Digital Technology. Government is very much interested in introducing Computer Technology in Class Room instruction in Teacher Education. Hence the Investigator was interested to know the level of Awareness on Digital techniques applying in classroom teaching for present generation among Teacher Educators.

STATEMENT OF THE PROBLEM

1. The important key words used in this problem were i) Awareness: Alertness, New Idea.
2. Digital Technology: The Technology which is used to change the method of Class Room Teaching with the help of Electronic machines and Computer,
3. Teacher Educators Teachers who are working in the Colleges of Education.

OVERVIEW OF THE STUDY ALREADY DONE

Asan(2003) studied on "Computer Technology Awareness by Elementary School Teachers: A Case Study from Turkey" and found that many Teachers were not computer users. At the same time Wheatley, (2003) also studied on increasing computer use in early childhood Teacher Education. The study was found that Teachers lacked a functional Computer Literacy Foundation to new Technology and skills. Nickish and Reinhard (1992) in their study

"Teacher Anxiety toward Computer Technology" found that Urban Teachers are used Computer often than Rural Teachers. Sengamalam @ Vanathi (2013) Studied on Awareness on e learning among M.Ed scholars under Bharathidasan University, found that the awareness of scholars whose major subject is Science was found to be superior to the scholars with Arts as major subject.

OBJECTIVES OF THE STUDY

The objectives of the study were i) to measure the level of Awareness on Digital Technology among Teacher Educators. ii) To measure the level of significant difference on the Awareness on Digital Technology among Male and Female, Rural and Urban, Science and Arts group Teacher Educators.

METHOD AND MATERIALS

It is the Normative Survey method. Investigator constructed a Tool Awareness on Digital Techniques applying in Classroom Teaching for present generation among Teacher Educators. That consists of 40 statements with different dimensions such as Computer in Teaching Learning, Power point Presentation and Internet, which have four point scale such a Strongly Agree, Agree, Disagree and Strongly Disagree. After the Development of the Questionnaire, the Investigator distributed it to Teacher Educators for validation. Their valuable ideas were taken care. Then the questionnaire was given to 10 Teacher Educators by Test - Retest method. The obtained r value 0.84 reveals that the tool is reliable one. Investigators randomly selected 100 Teacher Educators from various Colleges of Education in Perambalur and Trichy Districts.

ANALYSIS

The collected data was analysed by using different statistical technique like Mean, SD and 't' test. The results are given in the following Tables

TABLE. 15.1: Significant Difference on the Mean Scores of Male and Female Teacher Educators

S.No	Dimension	Gender	Mean	SD	t test	Remarks
1.	Total	Male Female	64.3 63.0	0.74 0.92	7.38	S
2.	CTL	Male Female	60.54 61.62	1.19 1.41	1.48	NS
3.	PPT	Male Female	65.04 61.24	3.89 0.98	6.43	S
4.	INT	Male Female	71.07 69.58	1.92 3.35	2.38	S

CTL – Computer in Teaching Learning **PPT** – Power Point Presentation
INT Internet **NS** - Not Significant S - Significant

From the above Table it is noted that the 't' values are significantly difference at 5% level of the Teacher Educators for Total, PPT(Power Point Presentation) and INT(Internet). Total, PPT (Power Point Presentation) and INT (Internet) the Mean score of Male Teacher Educators are higher than the Female Teacher Educators. In CTL(Computer in Teaching Learning) there is no significant difference at 5 % level of the Teacher Educators.

TABLE. 15.2: Significant Difference on the Mean Scores of Rural and Urban Teacher Educators

S.No	Dimension	Locality	Mean	SD	t test	Remarks
1.	Total	Rural Urban	64.7 63.07	0.837 0.823	5.46	S
2.	CTL	Rural Urban	60.74 63.18	1.61 0.989	1.69	NS
3.	PPT	Rural Urban	62.90 63.07	0.78 0.65	1.06	NS
4.	INT	Rural Urban	74.53 70.93	1.72 1.68	3.62	S

From the above Table, the calculated 't' values are revealing that there is no significant difference at 5% level for the dimensions CTL and PPT. But there exists significant difference at 5% level with respect to Total and INT. In the Total and INT the Mean score of the Rural Teacher Educators are higher having higher awareness on Digital Technology than the Urban Teacher Educators.

TABLE. 15.3: Significant Difference on the Mean Scores of Science and Arts Teacher Educators

S.No	Dimension	Subject	Mean	SD	t test	Remarks
1.	Total	Science Arts	63.83 64.31	0.929 0.779	1.21	NS
2.	CTL	Science Arts	62.43 61.28	1.06 1.11	4.79	S
3.	PPT	Science Arts	63.02 60.34	4.22 0.934	3.27	S
4.	INT	Science Arts	71.94 73.38	1.19 1.02	6.03	S

The Mean scores and the calculated 't ' values from the above table shows that there is significant difference in all the mean score of CTL, PPT and INT at 5% level except Total. It can be understood that the level Awareness on Digital Technology among Teacher Educators are good in CTL , PPT and INT.

RESULTS AND DISCUSSION

The salient findings of the study are i) All the Teacher Educators am having good Awareness on Digital Technology. ii) The Mean score of Male Teacher Educators are higher than the Female Teacher Educators towards Awareness on Digital Technology with respect to the dimensions such as Total, PPT and INT. iii) With regards to Locality, the Mean score of Rural Teacher Educators are higher than the Urban Teacher Educators towards Awareness on Digital Technology in Total and INT. iv) The Mean scores of Teacher Educators with respect to Science Subject are higher in CTL, PPT and Arts Teacher Educators are higher in INT.

The result shows that Gender, Locality and Subject of Teacher Educators were not the influencing factor in determining Awareness on Digital Technology. While considering the Gender, Male Teachers are having higher Awareness on Digital Technology than the Female Teachers. This is because Male Teacher Educators may have more time to work in the Computer but the Female Teachers have the commitment to look after their family. By this way Rural Teachers are having Good Awareness on Digital Technology than the Urban Teachers. This is due to the fact that Rural Teachers may show more interest to know about the new things. As well as Science Group Teacher Educators are show more awareness than Art Group Teacher Educators. It may be due to their subject knowledge.

RECOMMENDATIONS FOR POLICY MAKINGS

The result of this study shows that the Teacher Educators are having Good awareness on Digital Technology. Hence the usage of Computer must be increased to develop their practical knowledge. They are having more involvement in using Digital Technology in their class room Teaching. Effective teaching to promote better learning, proper orientation training Programme must be provided them to develop their knowledge in Digital Technology. The Government must ensure proper training to Teacher Educators to maintain Computers and Electronic things. Educational Authorities should create, improve and sustain the Awareness of Teacher Educators about Computer Knowledge. Teacher Educators should be encouraged by Administrators to use the stand alone Computer Applications in their Teachings. Using Internet application should be given special concentration, because, it empowers and enhance creativity. Digital Technology acts as a catalyst to support change in Teacher Pedagogy.

Conclusion

The Good Awareness on Computer Technology among Primary and Middle School Teachers will show the Conducing Climate towards Educational Technology. The Instruction through Computer has been making wonders in the Class Room Activities. Hence Teachers must have Awareness on Computer Technology to get success and enjoy their Professions.

❐

16

Relevant Effect.of C.based M.L.M. on Performance and Behaviour of H.S.S.inT.

Performance and behavioural outcome of the student is important aspects in school education here performance refers knowledge uplifted from the course of study. Behaviour outcome refers to social behaviour like responsible co-operation. Now a day complete is using in the entire field for the various purpose. In our education computer is used for giving instruction, administration and research. CAT, programmed instruction, PSI all is innovations in educational field to improve the performance. So the researcher has as her rightly chosen the study of the relevant effectiveness of computer based multimedia learning material on performance and behaviour outcome of high school students. The present study to find out the relevant effectiveness of computer based multimedia learning material on performance and behaviour outcome in Tindivanam Town. A samples of 100 respondents selected randomly were studied. A questionnaire method of survey was used to find out the effectiveness of computer based multimedia learning material on performance and behaviour outcome. The data were collected by using questionnaire as an instrument. Primary data were collected by conducting direct structured interview using questionnaire. All the respondents were asked the same questions in the same fashion and they were informed the purpose of study. T-test, One Way ANOVA and Correlation analysis was applied to test the hypotheses. The findings and observations are the result and outcome of the interpretations made during the study of analysis. The result found that there is a significant difference between traditional method and computer method of teaching.

Multimedia refers to any computer-mediated software or interactive application that integrates text, color, graphical images, animation, audio sound, and full motion video in a single application. Multimedia learning systems consist of animation and narration, which offer a potential venue for improving student understanding. Multimedia programme is an integral part of the educational technology. As a technique, it offers a high potential in application at different stages of education for the purpose of enhancing the teaching and learning processes, as is evident from the experience of developed countries.

The integration of multimedia technology into the communication environment has the potential to transform the students from passive recipients of information to active participants in a media-rich learning process. The introduction of multimedia or any other computer-based information technology is not intended to substitute a presenter. This new technology is intended to provide the presenter with a powerful tool that can greatly enhance communication by delivering a multisensory experience. With interactive multimedia technology, a teacher can communicate with the students by means of a presentation that becomes more than message-it becomes an active, exciting experience in a multisensory environment to create a multisensory experience. Multimedia reaches users in many different ways, enabling them to retain more knowledge and increase their understanding.

There are 4 steps in learning like attention, rehearsal, encoding and retrieval. A well designed multimedia application demands the simultaneous attention of several senses through dual encoding or the process of appealing to more than one sense simultaneously. Dual encoding facilitates and enhances the rehearsal process. Multimedia helps retrieval by associating sound, text and images with the concept being presented. Using text, images, animation and sound simultaneously greatly improves the students' retention of the knowledge and directs the students' attention to classroom (Louis, 2001).

Multimedia consists of the combination of video and movie clips and sound, text and graphic files all controlled by a piece of software and a computer which is equipped with a sound card, a video card, a CD-ROM drive and speakers or headphone. Sometimes, there is also a videodisk player, which is controlled by the software.

Computer based multimedia delivers information in a variety of ways but achieves its greatest effectiveness through interaction. In the first case, music and informative knowledge combine to convey the message. In the second case, technology provides a more effective presentation wherein information, images and sounds are technically and aesthetically integrated, focusing on a single specific purpose. The ability of students to work independently and to receive instruction suited to their needs and learning styles is inherently attractive.

REVIEW OF LITERATURE

Dalacosta et al. (2009) developed and studied the effectiveness of Multimedia **application with animated cartoons in teaching science in elementary education.** The results of the study provide evidence that the use of animated cartoons significantly increases the young students' knowledge and understanding of specific science concepts, which are normally difficult to comprehend and often cause misconceptions to them.

Jian Hu et al. (2009) investigated the effects of introducing a software program, named the Dental 3D Multimedia System (D3DM), into the education of a group of junior dental students in their preclinical practice. One group received their training program in the traditional way, unassisted by 3D technology. The second group received their training program in the traditional manner, but also used the D3DM to supplement their education. The results showed that the D3DM-assisted group achieved higher scores and also indicated that the usage of 3D multimedia PC software had a positive impact on several aspects of subjects' performance.

Kanmani and Radha (2009) studied the Effectiveness of CAI package in basic electronics teaching. There was a significant difference between the control and the experimental group students in attainment of knowledge level, understanding level, and application level objective in the gain scores. Hence, the experimental group students were better than the control group students in attainment of knowledge level, understanding level, and application level objective in the gain scores. It was inferred from the finding that the experimental treatment is effective to the students.

Korakakis et al. (2009) made a study on the **"3D visualization types in multimedia applications for science learning for 8th grade students in Greece".** The aim of the study was to determine whether the use of specific types of visualization (3D illustration, 3D animation, and interactive 3D animation) combined with narration and text, contributes to the learning process in science courses. The results indicated that multimedia applications with interactive 3D animations as well as with 3D animations do in fact increase the interest of students and make the material more appealing to them.

She, Hsiao-Ching and Chen, Yi-Zen (2009) examined how middle school students constructed their understanding of the mitosis and meiosis processes at a molecular level through multimedia learning materials presented in different interaction and sensory modality modes. The dependent variables included subjects' pre-test, post-test, and retention-test scores, showing their understanding of mitosis and meiosis process at molecular level. The results of the study showed that the group which used multimedia learning material has a greater amount of visual attention and consistent with their long term retained learning than the group which did not use the same. This study adds empirical evidence of a direct correlation between the length of eye fixation behavior and the depth of learning. Moreover, it provides insight into the multimedia effect on students' cognitive process through the use of eye fixation behavior evidence.

Anboucarassy (2010) studied the effectiveness of Multimedia in Teaching Biological Science to IX Standard students. The results of the study revealed that experiment group performed better than the control group due to the exposure of multimedia based learning. Thus multimedia helps the students to sustain their interest and also their retention power compared to the traditional method of teaching. The constant use of multimedia will make students understand more and achieve more in their academic achievement. Hence it was concluded that the multimedia approach is considered to be one of the best techniques for biology teaching at IX standard level.

Ponraj and Sivakumar (2010) studied the effectiveness of Computer-Assisted Instruction in Teaching Zoology in Relation to Learners' Personality. The major findings of the study indicated that achievement scores of experimental group students were higher than the control group students after the treatment.

Yusuf, Mudasiru and Afolabi, Adedeji (2010) investigated the effects of computer assisted instruction (CAI) on secondary school students' performance in biology. The findings of the study showed that the performance of students exposed to CAI either individually or cooperatively were better than their counterparts exposed to the conventional classroom instruction. Based on the research findings recommendations were made on the need to develop relevant CAI packages for teaching biology in Nigerian secondary schools.

OBJECTIVES

1. To measure behaviour and performance of high school student.
2. To assess effectiveness in performance of high school student
3. To assess effective in behaviuoral outcome of the high school student.
4. To assess effectiveness in traditional and multimedia method of teaching.

5. To find out relevant effectiveness of computer based multimedia learning material on performance and behaviour outcome.

HYPOTHESIS OF THE STUDY

High school students do not differ in their average level of relevant effectiveness of computer based on multimedia learning material on performance and behaviour outcome in traditional method and multimedia teaching of entire samples.

1. Respondents do not differ in their relevant effectiveness of computer based multimedia learning material on performance and behaviour outcome in pre test on the basis of groups.
2. Respondents do not differ in their relevant effectiveness of computer based multimedia learning material on performance and behaviour outcome in pre test on the basis of type of school.
3. Respondents do not differ in their relevant effectiveness of computer based multimedia learning material on performance and behaviour outcome in pre test on the basis of parent's education.
4. Respondents do not differ in their relevant effectiveness of computer based multimedia learning material on performance and behaviour outcome in pre test on the basis of parent's income.
5. Respondents do not differ in their relevant effectiveness of computer based multimedia learning material on performance and behaviour outcome in post test on the basis of type of school.
6. Respondents do not differ in their relevant effectiveness of computer based multimedia learning material on performance and behaviour outcome in post test on the basis of parent's education.
7. Respondents do not differ in their relevant effectiveness of computer based multimedia learning material on performance and behaviour outcome in post test on the basis of parent's income.

METHODOLOGY

The methodology adopted for the study is explained in detail. The sampling technique, size of the sample, variables of the study, description of the tool used and administration of tool are elaborated.

SAMPLING TECHNIQUE

The random sampling techniques used in the present study. The survey should cover all the aspects of the subject selected of the study others are inferred from a study of a sample group carefully selected to be representative of the total population. At time, the survey describes a limited population which is the only group under consideration. It involves a clearly defined problem and defined objectives. It requires expert and imaginative planning. Careful analysis and interpretation of the data gathered and logical and skillful reporting of the findings. There are different findings such as social surveys, market surveys. The survey method is applied to the analysis of existing social conditions including educational conditions and to the analysis of public opinion. So in this present study, the investigator has used stratified disposition random sampling method.

Sample

Samples of 100 high school students selected randomly were studied in Tindivanam Town. Out of these high schools as many as 5 higher secondary schools have been chosen by appropriate method. All the available high school students studying in each of this selected high school were chosen as sample. Stratified disposition random sampling technique has been used in the selection of the sample.

Data Collection

Primary data, required for the present research work were collected by conducting direct interviews using questionnaire. All the respondents were given sufficient information about the study. These respondents were provided with the same questionnaires. They were also informed that they have to answer in the same fashion.

Tools Used for the Study

Development of effectiveness of multimedia programme and Scale by the investigator. The scale for measuring the high school student's effectiveness of multimedia towards science in the study. This scale has as many as 25 statements of which 3 point scale method.

ANALYSIS AND INTERPRETATION

TABLE. 16.1: Showing the Mean, Standard Deviation of Relevant Effectiveness of Computer based Multimedia learning Material on Performance and behaviour Outcome in Pre and Post Test of Entire Samples

Groups	N	Mean	SD	r value
Pre test	100	14.79	2.69	0.346**
Post test	100	19.30	2.86	

Hypothesis

High school students do not differ in their average level of relevant effectiveness of computer based on multimedia learning material on performance and behaviour outcome in traditional method and multimedia teaching of entire samples.

The mean and standard deviation of relevant effectiveness of computer based multimedia learning material on performance and behaviour outcome scores of entire samples are 14.79 and 2.69 in pre test and 19.30 and 2.86 in post test. The mean score of all categories are lay in between (M ± 1σ) value. So it is concluded that average level of relevant effectiveness of computer based multimedia learning material on performance and behaviour outcome of entire samples.

TABLE. 16.2: Showing the Mean, Standard Deviation and T-Test for Relevant Effectiveness of Computer based Multimedia learning Material on Performance and Behaviour Outcome on the basis of Groups

Groups	Sample size	Mean	Standard Deviation	t-value	Level of Significance
Pre test	100	14.79	2.69	12.86	0.01 (Significant)
Post test	100	19.30	2.86		

Hypothesis

Respondents do not differ in their relevant effectiveness of computer based multimedia learning material on performance and behaviour outcome in pre test on the basis of groups.

The calculated t-value (12.86), which is significant at 0.01 level, confirms that there is a significant difference between relevant effectiveness of computer based multimedia learning material on performance and behaviour outcome on the basis of groups. So the null hypothesis is rejected and alternate hypothesis is accepted. Therefore it is concluded that pre test and post test groups differ in their effectiveness of computer based multimedia learning material on performance and behaviour outcome.

TABLE. 16.3: Showing mean, Standard Deviation and T-Value for Traditional Method among the High School Student on the basis of Type of School

Sl. No	Type of school	Sample size	Mean	Standard Deviation	t-value	Level of Significance
1	Government	75	14.73	2.71	0.37	0.716 (Not Significant)
2	Aided	25	14.96	2.67		

Hypothesis

Respondents do not differ in their relevant effectiveness of computer based multimedia learning material on performance and behaviour outcome in pre test on the basis of type of school.

The calculated t-value (0.37), which is not significant, confirms that there is a no significant difference between relevant effectiveness of computer based multimedia learning material on performance and behaviour outcome in pre test on the basis of type of school. So the null hypothesis is accepted and alternate hypothesis is rejected. Therefore it is concluded that government and aided school groups do not differ in their pre test score.

TABLE. 16.4: Showing mean, Standard Deviation and T-Value for Traditional Method among the High School Student on the basis of Parents Education

Sl. No	Parents education	Sample size	Mean	Standard Deviation	F-value	Level of Significance
1	School	86	14.82	2.75	0.58	0.560 (Not Significant)
2	Under graduate	8	14.13	2.03		
3	Post graduate	6	14.21	2.44		
	Total	**100**	**14.79**	**2.69**		

Hypothesis

Respondents do not differ in their relevant effectiveness of computer based multimedia learning material on performance and behaviour outcome in pre test on the basis of parents education.

The calculated F-value (0.58), which is not significant, confirms that there is a no significant difference between relevant effectiveness of computer based multimedia learning material on performance and behaviour outcome in pre test on the basis of parents education. So the null hypothesis is accepted and alternate hypothesis is rejected. Therefore it is concluded that different parents education students groups do not differ in their pre test score.

TABLE. 16.5: Showing mean, Standard Deviation and T-Value for Traditional Method among the High School Student on the basis of Parents Income

Sl. No	Parents income	Sample size	Mean	Standard Deviation	F-value	Level of Significance
1	Below Rs.50,000	70	14.51	2.53	1.56	0.215 (Not Significant)
2	Rs.50,000 – 2,00,000	24	15.50	3.09		
3	Above Rs.2,00,000	6	16.00	2.65		
	Total	**100**	**14.79**	**2.69**		

Hypothesis

Respondents do not differ in their relevant effectiveness of computer based multimedia learning material on performance and behaviour outcome in pre test on the basis of parents income.

The calculated F-value (1.56), which is not significant, confirms that there is a no significant difference between relevant effectiveness of computer based multimedia learning material on performance and behaviour outcome in pre test on the basis of parents income. So the null hypothesis is accepted and alternate hypothesis is rejected. Therefore it is concluded that different parents income students groups do not differ in their pre test score.

TABLE. 16.6: Showing mean, Standard Deviation and T-Value for Multimedia Method among the High School Student on the basis of Type of School

Sl. No	Type of school	Sample size	Mean	Standard Deviation	t-value	Level of Significance
1	Government	75	18.75	2.91	4.33	0.01 (Significant)
2	Aided	25	20.96	1.93		

Hypothesis

Respondents do not differ in their relevant effectiveness of computer based multimedia learning material on performance and behaviour outcome in post test on the basis of type of school.

The calculated t-value (4.33), which is significant at 0.01 level, confirms that there is a significant difference between relevant effectiveness of computer based multimedia learning material on performance and behaviour outcome in post test on the basis of type of school. So the null hypothesis is rejected and alternate hypothesis is accepted. Therefore it is concluded that aided school students (20.96) scored higher mean value than government school students (18.75).

TABLE. 16.7: Showing mean, Standard Deviation and T-Value for Multimedia Method among the High School Student on the basis of Parents Education

Sl. No	Parents education	Sample size	Mean	Standard Deviation	F-value	Level of Significance
1	School	86	19.34	2.87	3.19	0.01 (Significant)
2	Under graduate	8	16.75	3.01		
3	Post graduate	6	20.12	2.63		
	Total	**100**	**19.30**	**2.86**		

Hypothesis

Respondents do not differ in their relevant effectiveness of computer based multimedia learning material on performance and behaviour outcome in post test on the basis of parents education.

The calculated F-value (3.19), which is significant at 0.01 level, confirms that there is a significant difference between relevant effectiveness of computer based multimedia learning material on performance and behaviour outcome in post test on the basis of parents education. So the null hypothesis is rejected and alternate hypothesis is accepted. Therefore it is concluded that different parents education students groups differ in their post test score.

TABLE. 16.8: Showing mean, Standard Deviation and T-Value for Nultimedia Method among the High School Student on the basis of Parents Income

Sl. No	Parents income	Sample size	Mean	Standard Deviation	F-value	Level of Significance
1	Below Rs.50,000	70	19.11	2.64	3.29	0.01 (Significant)
2	Rs.50,000 – 2,00,000	24	20.04	3.24		
3	Above Rs.2,00,000	6	16.00	4.58		
	Total	**100**	**19.30**	**2.86**		

Hypothesis

Respondents do not differ in their relevant effectiveness of computer based multimedia learning material on performance and behaviour outcome in post test on the basis of parents income.

The calculated F-value (3.29), which is significant at 0.01 level, confirms that there is a significant difference between relevant effectiveness of computer based multimedia learning material on performance and behaviour outcome in post test on the basis of parents income. So the null hypothesis is rejected and alternate hypothesis is accepted. Therefore it is concluded that different parents income students groups differ in their post test score.

Findings

High school students differ in their average level of relevant effectiveness of computer based on multimedia learning material on performance and behaviour outcome in traditional method and multimedia teaching of entire samples.

1. Respondents differ in their relevant effectiveness of computer based multimedia learning material on performance and behaviour outcome in pre test on the basis of groups.
2. Respondents do not differ in their relevant effectiveness of computer based multimedia learning material on performance and behaviour outcome in pre test on the basis of type of school.
3. Respondents do not differ in their relevant effectiveness of computer based multimedia learning material on performance and behaviour outcome in pre test on the basis of parents education.
4. Respondents do not differ in their relevant effectiveness of computer based multimedia learning material on performance and behaviour outcome in pre test on the basis of parents income.
5. Respondents differ in their relevant effectiveness of computer based multimedia learning material on performance and behaviour outcome in post test on the basis of type of school.

6. Respondents differ in their relevant effectiveness of computer based multimedia learning material on performance and behaviour outcome in post test on the basis of parents education.
7. Respondents differ in their relevant effectiveness of computer based multimedia learning material on performance and behaviour outcome in post test on the basis of parents income.

Conclusion

In the present study, the researcher arrive the following conclusion based on the findings. In the present study, science students have relevant effectiveness of computer based multimedia learning material on performance and behaviour outcome of high school students in Tindivanam Town when compared with other students. The researcher framed objectives and hypotheses on the basis of the above context. 100 samples were selected randomly. A standard questionnaire was used to collect the relevant data. After collecting the data they were analyzed using statistical tools such as t-test and ANOVA in the both groups (pre and post test). The result concluded that the all the science students of average level of relevant effectiveness of computer based multimedia learning material on performance and behaviour outcome.

❒

17

Awareness on Digital Tec. Applying in C.T. for Present Generation among T.E.

Modernization is generally regarded as a process of change of traditional society into a society based on technology. As Teaching has entered the Digital age over the last several years, Technology in the Classroom is an area that all Teachers and Students are Embracing. For Teachers who have taught many years before this can be a challenging one. There are many Computer lesson plans, CDs, DVDs, audio e -books and videos available that will help in the transition. Digital Technology in the Classroom involves a lot of time and focus in its infancy, but with the Computer Lesson plans mentioned, it will develop into a fun and creative learning experience for Students and new and exciting challenges for Teachers. The incorporation of Digital technology in the education sector is important to meet the challenges presented by new trends, especially with the Global Communication of Knowledge. It is essential that the Students become familiar with the concept and use of Computer Technology in order to equip them for future job market. Similarly, the teacher can achieve better quality in Teaching Methodology.

RATIONALE OF THE STUDY

Computer plays key role in Education. Learning through Computer is an interesting affair. Now–a-days Digital Technology in Education has become the essential part of the system. In fact Teacher must well aware of the potentiality of the Digital Technology. Government is very much interested in introducing Computer Technology in Class Room instruction in Teacher Education. Hence the Investigator was interested to know the level of Awareness on Digital techniques applying in classroom teaching for present generation among Teacher Educators.

STATEMENT OF THE PROBLEM

The important key words used in this problem were i) Awareness: Alertness, New Idea.

1. Digital Technology: The Technology which is used to change the method of Class Room Teaching with the help of Electronic machines and Computer,
2. Teacher Educators Teachers who are working in the Colleges of Education.

OVERVIEW OF THE STUDY ALREADY DONE

Askin Asan (2003) studied on "Computer Technology Awareness by Elementary School Teachers: A Case Study from Turkey" and found that many Teachers were not computer users. At the same time Wheatley, (2003) also studied on increasing computer use in early childhood Teacher Education. The study was found that Teachers lacked a functional Computer Literacy Foundation to new Technology and skills. Nickish and Reinhard (1992) in their study "Teacher Anxiety toward Computer Technology" found that Urban Teachers are used Computer often than Rural Teachers. Sengamalam @ Vanathi (2013) Studied on Awareness on e learning among M.Ed scholars under Bharathidasan University, found that the awareness of scholars whose major subject is Science was found to be superior to the scholars with Arts as major subject.

OBJECTIVES OF THE STUDY

The objectives of the study were i) To measure the level of Awareness on Digital Technology among Teacher Educators. ii) To measure the level of significant difference on the Awareness on Digital Technology among Male and Female, Rural and Urban, Science and Arts group Teacher Educators.

METHOD AND MATERIALS

It is the Normative Survey method. Investigator constructed a Tool Awareness on Digital Techniques applying in Classroom Teaching for present generation among Teacher Educators. That consists of 40 statements with different dimensions such as Computer in Teaching Learning, Power point Presentation and Internet, which have four point scale such a Strongly Agree, Agree, Disagree and Strongly Disagree. After the Development of the Questionnaire, the Investigator distributed it to Teacher Educators for validation. Their valuable ideas were taken care. Then the questionnaire was given to 10 Teacher Educators by Test - Retest method. The obtained r value 0.84 reveals that the tool is reliable one. Investigators randomly selected 100 Teacher Educators from various Colleges of Education in Perambalur and Trichy Districts.

ANALYSIS

The collected data was analysed by using different statistical technique like Mean, SD and 't' test. The results are given in the following Tables

TABLE. 17.1: Significant Difference on the Mean Scores of Male and Female Teacher Educators

S. No	Dimension	Gender	Mean	SD	t test	Remarks
1.	**Total**	Male Female	64.3 63.0	0.74 0.92	**7.38**	S
2.	**CTL**	Male Female	60.54 61.62	1.19 1.41	1.48	NS
3.	**PPT**	Male Female	65.04 61.24	3.89 0.98	**6.43**	S
4.	**INT**	Male Female	71.07 69.58	1.92 3.35	**2.38**	S

CTL – Computer in Teaching Learning **PPT** – Power Point Presentation
INT Internet **NS** - Not Significant **S** - Significant

From the above Table it is noted that the 't' values are significantly difference at 5% level of the Teacher Educators for Total, PPT(Power Point Presentation) and INT(Internet) . Total, PPT (Power Point Presentation) and INT (Internet) the Mean score of Male Teacher Educators are higher than the Female Teacher Educators. In CTL(Computer in Teaching Learning) there is no significant difference at 5 % level of the Teacher Educators.

TABLE. 17.2: Significant Difference on the Mean Scores of Rural and Urban Teacher Educators

S.No	Dimension	Locality	Mean	SD	t test	Remarks
1.	**Total**	Rural Urban	64.7 63.07	0.837 0.823	**5.46**	S
2.	**CTL**	Rural Urban	60.74 63.18	1.61 0.989	1.69	NS
3.	**PPT**	Rural Urban	62.90 63.07	0.78 0.65	1.06	NS
4.	**INT**	Rural Urban	74.53 70.93	1.72 1.68	**3.62**	S

From the above Table, the calculated 't' values are reveal that there is no significant difference at 5% level for the dimensions CTL and PPT. But there exists significant difference at 5% level with respect to Total and INT. In the Total and INT the Mean score of the Rural Teacher Educators are higher having higher awareness on Digital Technology than the Urban Teacher Educators.

TABLE. 17.3: Significant Difference on the Mean Scores of Science and Arts Teacher Educators

S.No	Dimension	Subject	Mean	SD	t test	Remarks
1.	**Total**	Science Arts	63.83 64.31	0.929 0.779	1.21	NS
2.	**CTL**	Science Arts	62.43 61.28	1.06 1.11	**4.79**	S
3.	**PPT**	Science Arts	63.02 60.34	4.22 0.934	**3.27**	S
4.	**INT**	Science Arts	71.94 73.38	1.19 1.02	**6.03**	S

The Mean scores and the calculated 't ' values from the above table shows that there is significant difference in all the mean score of CTL, PPT and INT at 5% level except Total. It can be understood that the level Awareness on Digital Technology among Teacher Educators are good in CTL , PPT and INT.

RESULTS AND DISCUSSION

The salient findings of the study are i) All the Teacher Educators are having good Awareness on Digitaol Technology. ii) The Mean score of Male Teacher Educators are higher than the Female Teacher Educators towards Awareness on Digital Technology with respect to the dimensions such as Total, PPT and INT. iii) With regards to Locality, the Mean score of Rural Teacher Educators are higher than the Urban Teacher Educators towards Awareness on Digital Technology in Total and INT. iv) The Mean scores of Teacher Educators with respect to Science Subject are higher in CTL, PPT and Arts Teacher Educators are higher in INT.

The result shows that Gender, Locality and Subject of Teacher Educators were not the influencing factor in determining Awareness on Digital Technology. While considering the Gender, Male Teachers are having higher Awareness on Digital Technology than the Female Teachers. This is because Male Teacher Educators may have more time to work in the Computer but the Female Teachers have the commitment to look after their family. By this way Rural Teachers are having Good Awareness on Digital Technology than the Urban Teachers. This is due to the fact that Rural Teachers may show more interest to know about the new things. As well as Science Group Teacher Educators are show more awareness than Art Group Teacher Educators. It may be due to their subject knowledge.

RECOMMENDATIONS FOR POLICY MAKINGS

The result of this study shows that the Teacher Educators are having Good awareness on Digital Technology. Hence the usage of Computer must be increased to develop their practical knowledge. They are having more involvement in using Digital Technology in their class room Teaching. Effective teaching to promote better learning, proper orientation training Programme must be provided them to develop their knowledge in Digital Technology. The Government must ensure proper training to Teacher Educators to maintain Computers and Electronic things. Educational Authorities should create, improve and sustain the Awareness of Teacher Educators about Computer Knowledge. Teacher Educators should be encouraged by Administrators to use the stand alone Computer Applications in their Teachings. Using Internet application should be given special concentration, because, it empowers and enhance creativity. Digital Technology acts as a catalyst to support change in Teacher Pedagogy.

Conclusion

The Good Awareness on Computer Technology among Primary and Middle School Teachers will show the Conducing Climate towards Educational Technology. The Instruction through Computer has been making wonders in the Class Room Activities. Hence Teachers must have Awareness on Computer Technology to get success and enjoy their Professions.

❐

18

Learning Styles of Higher Secondary Students

The act or experience of one that learns. Knowledge or skill acquired by instruction or study. Modification of a behavioral tendency by experience (as exposure to conditioning). Adapted from How Learning Works by Ambrose et al.: an engagingly written, evidence-based text, well-illustrated by practical examples, and a book well worth your time, as a TA and as a student.

As teachers, our goal is to encourage learning in our classrooms. But what is learning, and what principles or factors affect how our students learn? In this section, we provide you with the very basics of what learning is, how and when it occurs, and how to structure your lessons to maximize student learning.

There are three components to the definition of Learning:

1. **"Learning is a process, not a product."** Exam scores and term papers are measures of learning, but they are not the process of learning itself.
2. **"Learning is a change in knowledge, beliefs, behaviors or attitudes.** This change requires time, particularly when one is dealing with changes to core beliefs, behaviors, and attitudes. Don't interpret a lack of sea change in your students' beliefs or attitudes immediately following a lesson as a lack of learning on their part, but instead, consider that such a change will take time – perhaps a few weeks, perhaps until the end of the term, or even longer.
3. **"Learning is not something done to students, but something that students themselves do."** If you have ever carefully planned a lesson,

only to find that your students just didn't "get it," consider that your lesson should be designed not just to impart knowledge but also to lead students through the process of their own learning.

Learning is the process by which one acquires, ingests, and stores or accepts information. Our experiences with learned information compose our bodies of knowledge. Learning is a process unique to each individual. Some learn quickly, scanning the information and mastering the concept or skill seemingly effortlessly. Others stumble while processing information, taking longer to grasp the concept or requiring numerous exposures over a sustained period of time. Some individuals store the information they've learned indefinitely, cementing it in their memories. Others find that the information they've learned slips away rapidly. Some learn best through text, others through practice, some through hearing. Learning styles are as unique and varied as our personalities. Learning is a lifelong endeavor. As long as one remains engaged in life, learning does not cease.

Until recently most people took learning styles for granted and left them to instinct. Realization that studying how learning should come before everything else is spreading in the world of education skill in this field can multiply efficiency.

The use of higher level work skills can bring improvement in almost all fields. Improvement in athletic field and industrial productivity have been achieved in the way. Everyone is familiar with the difference in output of a self-taught typist who uses one finger of each hand and an expert who was taught the tough system. Other experiments has shown that the level of performance on such tasks as card sorting, pitch discrimination and puzzle solving is affected by the method employed and the limit to performance might be improved of better work was used.

These findings on effects of work methods on levels of performance led to the significant theoretical contribution to theories regarding the causes of individual difference in competence. It was long assumed that these differences were primarily due to two factors. (1) Learning and (2) Amount of training in a task. Dr. Seashare after studying may findings on effects of work method concluded that method of work was a third variable in instruction. It is found that new levels in achievement are possible by improving the learning styles.

Both in common speech and educational literature the word "Read" is used to designate a wide variety of learned activities from the socially undesirable to the highly ethnical, form bodily skill, such as walking to mental activities such as learning of critical thinking and from specified abilities to generalized attitudes. The meaning of learning includes the ideal of facility in the performance of an act, combined with a persisting inclination towards the repetition of the act.

As Bagley has said "To teach a child to study effectively is to do that most valuable thing that could be done to help him adjust himself to any environment of modern civilized life into which they live.

In 1917 strays and Newsworthy declared "Many teachers have taught subjects, but not how to study subjects, the latter is more important". H.R. Bhatia says, "unless opportunities for doing and respecting things are afforded to children it is futile to expect them to form habits". Sevmors and exhortations may help children to acquire normal vocabulary but not normal character. Percepta in the formation of learning unless children are afforded actual practice in those modes behaviour.

REVIEW OF LITERATURE

Mary Lou Koran, John J. Koran (2006), conducted a study "Interaction of Learner aptitudes with question packing in learning from prose, he suggested that, in some cases, reduction in certain information Processing requirements may actually be an important prerequisite to affective utilization of other aptitudes (learning).

The over-all means used in the analysis are presented, both low and high aptitude students in "favourable" classrooms had higher achievements scores than the two groups in 'unfavourable' classroom. This contexts effect was present to some extent in both third and fourth grade class room aptitude, third grade students. It appears that being in a classroom with many high-aptitude students is beneficial for low-aptitude students and some high-aptitude students as well".

K.S Kahlon and Vinod Uppalo, (2007) studied on "women's aptitude and achievement in Relation to achievement motivation.

The Result of the present investigation fully support the hypotheses on the basis of which the study had been undertaken.

1. There is significant, but imperfect relationship between aptitude (learning style) and academic achievement.
2. Discrepancy between aptitude (Learning style) and achievement bears no relationship with ability.
3. Discrepancy between aptitude (Learning Style) and achievement bears significant relationship with academic achievement.
4. Discrepancy between aptitude and achievement bears significant relationship with achievement motivation. That is, high achievement motivation goes with positive discrepancy where as low achievement motivation accounts for negative discrepancy"

Robert B. Burnes (2012) conducted a study on "The Relation of Aptitudes of Learning at different Points in the time during Instruction: The result of this study suggested that some aptitude-learning relations are not stable over time and that his instability is exhibited in different aptitudes being required at different points in time during instruction. These findings supported most of the Junior evidence examining aptitude correlates at different stages of learning and did not support the assumption made in ATI Research that aptitudes relate equally to learning for the during of treatment"

Moraddwaj Varma (2013) conducted a study on "Comparative achievement in science of Tharu Tribals and other at high school level. He found, that the achievement of Tharu tribals is lower than that of the non-tharus in all the three science subjects were significant at .01 level".

In Jamur (2013) made a study in Patna in relationship between study habits and achievement. His study showed a correlation of 0.51 between study habits and achievement of students and a correlation of 0.144 between study habits and intelligence.

OBJECTIVES

1. To study the higher secondary learning styles in Biological science.
2. To know the higher secondary different methods learning styles in Biological science.
3. To find out the higher secondary factors learning styles in Biological science.

METHODOLOGY

The methodology adopted for the study is explained in detail. The sampling technique, size of the sample, variables of the study, description of the tool used and administration of tool are elaborated.

Sample

The sample selected for the present study is 100 higher secondary students in Villupuram district. Random sampling technique was used for the selection of sample.

Data Collection

Primary data, required for the present research work were collected by conducting direct interviews using questionnaire. All the respondents were given sufficient information about the Project work. These respondents were provided with the same questionnaires. They were also informed that they have to answer in the same fashion.

Tools used in the Study

SOLAT Tool of learning style D. Venketraman (1986) consists of 25 items. The learning style comprises 5 categories.

1. Verbal (1 to 5 items)
2. Content preference (6 to 10 items)
3. Class preference (11 to 15 items)
4. Learning preference (16 to 20 items)
5. Interest (20 to 25 items)

Scoring Procedure

The maximum score that a student obtains is 50 the minimum score that a student gain is 25.

Each item has two alternatives. If the student chooses the First alternative one mark is given. If the student chooses Second alternative the student it secures 2 marks. The first alternative of an item indicates the use of Right hemisphere of the brain and the second alternative of an item indicates the use of left hemisphere of the brain.

Tool validity and Reliability

The main attributes needed to be considered regarding a good tool are validity and reliability.

Validity: A measuring instrument is said to be valid if it measures what it purpose to measure. Validity may be defined as the extent to which an instrument or a test does the job derived of it.

The kind of validity and the extent or degrees to which it should be established are the major consideration while establishing validity.

In the present study the researcher found out the content validity. Content validity gives the logical evidence that the content of the items of a test is suitable for the purpose for which the test is designed and used. Content validity is established is 0.549.

Reliability

The efficiency of measuring the different items are called on aspect of reliability. Reliability determined test-retest method and it is found to be validity of the tool is (0.82).

HYPOTHESIS

1. The level of learning styles among higher secondary students on the basis of their demographic variables.
2. The level of different method learning styles among higher secondary students on the basis of their demographic variables.

3. The level of factors learning styles among higher secondary students on the basis of their demographic variables.

ANALYSIS AND INTERPRETATION

TABLE. 18.1: Showing the Stepwise Regression Analysis Predicting learning Styles among Higher Secondary Students and Demographic Variables

Sl. No	Step/Source	Unstandardized Coefficients Beta	Std. Error	Standardized Coefficients Beta Beta	Step t	P
1.	Gender	1.342	0.343	1.245	5.432	0.01
2.	Locality	1.224	0.392	0.269	6.641	0.01
3.	Family Income	1.924	0.549	0.149	4.142	0.01
4.	Father Education	2.334	0.667	0.108	5.339	0.01

* P < 0.01

Four variables viz Gender, Locality, Family income and Father Education have significantly contributed for predicting the learning styles among higher secondary students. The Gender seems to be 5.432, Locality seems to be 6.641, Family income seems to be 4.142 and Father education seems to be 5.339. The predictive value of these variables separately is 0.01.

TABLE. 18.2: Showing the Stepwise Regression Analysis Predicting Different Method learning Styles and Demographic Variables

Sl. No	Step/Source	Unstandardized Coefficients Beta	Std. Error	Standardized Coefficients Beta Beta	Step t	P
1.	Type of Family	1.133	0.505	0.434	2.246	0.01
2.	Religion	1.248	0.466	0.782	2.677	0.01
3.	Community	1.792	0.683	0.646	2.625	0.01
4.	Birth Place	2.338	0.670	0.954	3.490	0.01

* P < 0.01

Four variables viz Type of family, Religion, Community and Birth place have significantly contributed for predicting the method learning styles. The first variable Type of family seems to be 2.246, Religion seems to be 2.677, Community seems to be 2.625 and Birth place seems to be 3.490. The predictive value of these variables separately is 0.01.

TABLE. 18.3: Showing the Stepwise Regression Analysis Predicting Factors learning Styles among Higher Secondary Students and Demographic Variables

Sl. No	Step/Source	Unstandardized Coefficients Beta	Std. Error	Standardized Coefficients Beta Beta	Step t	P
1.	Gender	5.195	1.030	0.824	5.041	0.01
2.	Family Monthly Income	1.809	0.451	0.443	4.016	0.01

* P < 0.01

Two variables viz Gender and Family Monthly Income have significantly contributed for predicting the factors learning styles among higher secondary. The first variable Gender seems to be 5.195, when paired with the second variable Family monthly income is 1.809. The predictive value of these variables separately is 0.01.

TALBe. 18.4: Showing the Correlation between the learning Styles of Higher Secondary Students and Demographic Variables

Factors	Learning styles of higher secondary students
Gender	0.579*
Locality	0.782**
Family Income	0.591*
Father Education	0.572*
Type of Family	0.824**

* Significant at 0.01 level ** Significant at 0.05 level

Learning styles of higher secondary students is positively and significantly related to Gender (0.579), Locality (0.782), Family Income (0.591), Father Education (0.572) and Type of family (0.824). So the direct relationship between the Learning styles of higher secondary students and demographic variables.

Conclusion

The present study aims to find out the higher secondary students learning styles. The researcher framed objectives and hypotheses on the basis of the above context. The research was carried out in 100 samples based randomly. A questionnaire constructed by R was used to collect the relevant data. After collecting the data they were analyzed using statistical tools such as Regression and Correlation analysis. The result concluded that students have average level of learning styles at Higher Secondary level in Biological science in Villupuram District.

❒

19

Relation between Study Habits and Academic Achievement of PUC Students

The present study examined the impact of study habits of students in Chitradurga city, Karnataka, India in relation to Academic achievement, Gender and Faculty. The main objectives were to analyze the study habits of PUC students and to compare it in relation to Academic- Achievement, Gender and Faculty. The research design is quantitative. The sample was selected randomly out of 180 students- 90 were boys and 90 were girls. Out of these 180 students- 60 were from Arts faculty, 60 from Science and 60 from Commerce Faculty. The questionnaire was administered for collecting data from the students and t-test and Pearson Correlation statistical methods was used for analysis of data. It was found that there is no significant difference in Mean study habit in relation to gender, and faculties such as Arts, Science and Commerce but there is a significant relationship between study habits and academic achievement of PUC students."

Study habits are a well-planned and deliberate pattern of study which has attained a form of consistency on the part of the students toward understanding academic subjects and passing at examination. Study habits determine the academic achievement of students to a great extent. Both study habits and academic achievement are interrelated and dependent on each other. There are students who come from different environment, localities etc. and have different levels of academic achievement i.e., high and low. They also differ in the pattern of study habits. Some students have better study habits while the others have poor. Better the study habits, better is the academic achievement. Academic achievement means how much knowledge the individual has acquired from the school. Academic achievement of the students is determined by their study habits. Study habits and academic achievement are very essential for research worker and educationists to know that every child whether he is gifted, backward etc. should be educated in their own way. But if children possess good study habits they can show performance in academics and in every situation and if children's do not possess good study habits they cannot excel in life. It is the study habits which help the learner in obtaining Meaningful and desirable knowledge. Good study habits act as a strong weapon for the students to excel in life.

Need and Importance of Study

Study habits play a very important role in bringing about the better academic achievement. The study could bring to light the importance of study habits which are the major contributors of academic achievement. The primary aim of this study was to examine the effect of study habit on students' academic achievement. This general aim is expressed in the following specific objectives which are to: Assess the study habit of students in students; Compare the academic achievement of students who have developed a study habit and those who do not have study habit; Examine factors influencing students study habit; Investigate the effect of study habit on student's academic achievement.

Objectives of the Study

1. To study the difference in study habits of arts and science students.
2. To study the difference in study habits of science and commerce students.
3. To study the difference in study habits of arts and commerce students.
4. To study the difference in study habits of male and female students.
5. To study the difference in academic achievement of male and female students.
6. To study the difference in academic achievement of arts and science students.
7. To study the difference in academic achievement of arts and commerce students.
8. To study the difference in academic achievement of science and commerce students.
9. To study the correlation between study habits and academic achievement of students.

Hypothesis of the Study

1. There is no significant difference in study habits of arts and science students.
2. There is no significant difference in study habits of science and commerce students.
3. There is no significant difference in study habits of arts and commerce students.
4. There is no significant difference in study habits of male and female students.
5. There is no significant difference in academic achievement of male and female students.
6. There is no significant difference in academic achievement of arts and science students.
7. There is no significant difference in academic achievement of arts and commerce students.
8. There is no significant difference in academic achievement of science and commerce Students.
9. There is no significant correlation between study habits and academic achievement of Students.

Variables of the study

The variables considered are study habits, academic achievement, Gender and Faculty (Science, Commerce and Arts).

Sampling Technique

For the present study Simple Random Sampling technique was used to select 180 PUC students from different colleges in Chitradurga City, Karnataka State, India. Out of the Sample of 180 students, 90 were Male and 90 were Female and also maintained the equal stream Ratio of students from Arts 60, Science 60 and Commerce 60 students.

Tool: Following tools were used

1. Study habit inventory developed by M. Mukhopadhayay and D.N.Sansanwal (1963)
2. For academic achievement investigator collected the I year PUC examination marks of Graduation students from college records.

Statistical Techniques

In pursuance of objectives of the study and in order to test the research hypothesis set up, the't'- test and Pearson Correlation was used.

Analysis Interpretation of Data

The Objectives and Hypothesis wise analysis was done

Objective-1

To study the difference in study habits of Arts and Science students.

Hypothesis-1

"There is no significant difference in study habits of Arts and Science students."

TABLE3 19.1: Shows Mean, SD, and't' Value of Study Habits of Arts and Science Students

Group	Sample	Mean	SD	t-value	Significant at 0.05 level
Arts students 'study habits	60	64.66	7.1	.031	Not significant
Science students' study habits	60	68.64	7.4		

The above table reveals that the obtained'-value 0.031 which is less than the theoretical value 1.98.The obtained value of't' is not significant at 0.05 level. Hence the Null Hypothesis is accepted and it is concluded that, "There is no significant difference in study habits of arts and science students."

Objective-2.

To study the difference in Study Habits of Science and Commerce students.

Hypothesis-2

"There is no significant difference in Study habits of Science and Commerce Students."

TABLE. 19.2: Shows Mean, SD, and't' Value of Study Habits of Science and Commerce Students

Group	Sample	Mean	SD	t-value	Significant at 0.05 level
Science students 'study habits	60	68.64	7.4	0.40	Not significant
Commerce students' study habits	60	64.2	6.9		

The above table reveals that the obtained 't'-value 0.40 which is less than the theoretical value 1.98.The obtained value of't' is not significant at 0.05 level. Hence the Null Hypothesis is accepted and it is concluded that, "There is no significant difference in study habits of science and commerce students."

Objective-3

To study the difference in study habits of Arts and Commerce students.

Hypothesis-3

"There is no significant difference in study habits of Arts and Commerce Students."

TABLE. 19.3: Shows Mean, SD, and't' Values of Study Habits of Arts and Commerce Students

Group	Sample	Mean	SD	t-value	Significant at 0.05 level
Arts students' study habits	60	64.66	7.1	.032	Not significant
Commerce students' study habits	60	64.2	6.9		

The above table reveals that the obtained't'-value .032 which is less than the theoretical value 1.97.The obtained value of 't' is not significant at 0.05 level. Hence the Null Hypothesis is accepted and it is concluded that, "There is no significant difference in study habits of Arts and Commerce students."

Objective-4

To study the difference in study habits of Male and Female students.

Hypothesis-4

There is no significant difference in study habits of Male and Female students.'

TABLE. 19.4: Shows Mean, SD, and't' Values of Study Habits of Male and Female Students

Group	Sample	Mean	SD	t-value	Significant at 0.05 level
Male students' study habits	90	67.8	8.1	1.79	Not significant
Female students' study habits	90	66.2	7.6		

The above table reveals that the obtained't'-value 1.79 which is less than the theoretical value 1.97.The obtained value of 't' is not significant at 0.05 level. Hence the Null Hypothesis is accepted and it is concluded that, "There is no significant difference in study habits of male and female students.

Objective-5.

To study the difference in academic achievement of Male and Female students.

Hypothesis -5.

"There is no significant difference in academic achievement of Male and Female students."

TABLE. 19.5: Shows Mean, SD, and't' Values of Academic Achievement of Male and Female Students

Group	Sample	Mean	SD	t-value	Significant at 0.05 level
Male students' Academic Achievement	90	53.8	14.4	0.28	Not significant
Female students' Academic Achievement	90	55.2	14.6		

The above table reveals that the obtained't'-value 0.28 which is less than the theoretical value 1.97.The obtained value of 't' is not significant at 0.05 level. Hence the Null Hypothesis is accepted and it is concluded that, "There is no significant difference in academic achievement of male and female students."

Objective- 6

To study the difference in academic achievement of Arts and Science students.

Hypothesis-6

There is no significant difference in academic achievement of Arts and Science Students.

TABLE. 19.6: Shows Mean, SD, and't' Values of Academic Achievement of Arts and Science Students

Group	Sample	Mean	SD	t-value	Significant at 0.05 level
Arts students' Academic Achievement	60	47.8	13.4	3.21**	significant
Science students' Academic Achievement	60	54.2	11.6		

** Significant at 0.05 level

The above table reveals that the obtained 't'-value 3.21 is greater than the theoretical value of 1.98.The obtained value of't' is significant at 0.05 level. Hence the Null Hypothesis is rejected and it is formulated that "There is a significant difference in academic achievement of arts and science students." It was also found that girls and boys differ significantly in their study habits and academic achievement. (Singh Y.G., 2011). It can be inferred that there may be good co-relation in Study habits and academic achievement.

Objective-7

To study the difference in academic achievement of Arts and Commerce students.

Hypothesis-7

"There is no significant difference in academic achievement of Arts and Commerce students."

TABLE. 19.7: Shows Mean, SD, and't' Values of Academic Achievement of Arts and Commerce Students

Group	Sample	Mean	SD	t-value	Significant at 0.05 level
Arts students' Academic Achievement	60	47.8	13.4	3.81**	significant
Commerce students Academic Achievement	60	53.4	10.4		

** Significant at 0.05 level

The above table reveals that the obtained't'-value 3.81 is greater than the theoretical value of 1.98.The obtained value of 't' is significant at 0.05 level. Hence the Null Hypothesis is rejected and it is formulated that "There is no significant difference in academic achievement of arts and commerce students." It was also found that girls and boys differ significantly in their study habits and academic achievement. (Singh Y.G., 2011). It can be inferred that there may be good co-relation in Study habits and academic achievement.

Objective-8

To study the difference in academic achievement of Science and Commerce Students.

Hypothesis-8

"There is no significant difference in academic achievement of Science and Commerce students."

TABLE. 19.8: Shows Mean, SD, and't' Values of Academic Achievement of Science and Commerce Students

Group	Sample	Mean	SD	t-value	Significant at 0.05 level
science students' Academic Achievement	60	54.2	11.6	1.81	Not significant
Commerce students Academic Achievement	60	53.4	10.4		

The above table reveals that the obtained't'-value 1.81 which is less than the theoretical value 1.98.The obtained value of 't' is not significant at 0.05 level. Hence the Null Hypothesis is accepted and it is concluded that, "There is no significant difference in academic achievement of science and commerce students."

Objective-9

To study the relationship between Study habits and Academic achievement of Graduation students.

Hypothesis-9

"There is no significant relationship between study habits and academic Achievement of students."

TABLE. 19.9: Shows'r' Values of Study Habits and Academic Achievement of PUC Students

Group	Sample	Mean	SD	r-value	Significant at 0.05 level
PUC students' study Habits	180	65.2	9.6	3.42**	significant
PUC students' Academic Achievement	180	54.4	13.4		

**Significant at 0.05 level

The above table shows that the obtained r-value 3.42 is greater than the theoretical value 0.138.The obtained value of't' is significant at 0.05 level. Hence the Null Hypothesis is rejected and stated new hypothesis "There is a significant relationship between study habits and academic achievement of PUC students." There is a positive co-relation between study habits and academic achievement of students. It was also found that there exists relationship between Study Habits and Academic Achievement of Higher Secondary Students (Singh Y.G., 2011).

Conclusion

The present study has implication for the teacher and parents that they should encourage students particularly boys and girls with poor academic performance have better study habits which is essential for their survival in this competitive world. They should take also special care for the development of the better study habit. This research indicated that students can acquire efficient studying skills by Means of Curriculum for Developing Efficient Studying Skills and they increase their academic achievements thanks to these studying habits. In this sense, if quality of education is desired to be increased, students with high level of academic achievements are intended and growing youth is expected to compete with the young population of other states with the effect of globalization, it is necessary to make students acquire efficient studying skills. ❐

20

Upgrading Employability Skills of Teachers in the Digital Era

Blended learning, as a new approach to education, is rapidly being adopted by educational institutions for the purpose of teacher education or teacher training. Blended learning promises effectively boost the core of teaching and learning (Gómez & Igado, 2008). O Garrison & Kanuka, (2004) indicate that it can provide the learner with higher levels of learning. Blended learning environment provides a multi-faceted, student focused and technology integrated teaching and learning. Success of Blended Learning practice depends on the attitude of the teachers towards blended learning. Moreover, over the recent years, blended learning approach has been the fastest- growing trend among many educational settings. Many educational settings have changed their delivery methods to blended programs to take advantage of the best pedagogical techniques of mixing online and face-to-face learning (Godambe, Picciano, Schroeder, & Schweber, 2004). Due to benefits that blended learning programs such as maximizes effectiveness, foster the quality of teacher-learner interaction, the present study was carried out to find out the attitude of prospective teachers towards blended learning. 150 samples of prospective teachers were taken for the study. From the study it was found out that, the prospective teachers have high positive attitude towards Blended Learning. There is no significant difference between age group, Arts and

Science, undergraduates and postgraduates, studied online courses, computer skills, locality studied internet usage, day scholars and hostelites. Prospective teachers below the age group 25, Science, undergraduates, having computer skills, using internets for their studies, urban, day scholars have more positive attitude towards blended learning than their counterparts.

Blended learning environment integrates the advantages of e-learning method with some advantageous aspects of traditional method, such as face-to-face interaction. Blended learning brings traditional physical classes with elements of virtual education together (Finn & Bucceri, 2004). Brown (2003) stated that blended learning supports all the benefits of e-learning including cost reductions, time efficiency and location convenience for the learner as well as the essential one-on-one personal understanding and motivation that face to face instructions presents. Singh & Reed (2001) defined blended learning as a learning program where more than one delivery mode is being used with the objective of optimizing the learning outcome and cost of program delivery. Therefore, Singh (2003) proposed to refine this definition as "blended learning focuses on optimizing achievement of learning objectives by applying the "right" personal learning technologies to watch the "right" personal learning style to transfer the "right" skills to the "right" person at the "right" time. Blended learning is described by Thorne (2003) as "a way of meeting the challenges of tailoring learning and development to the needs of individuals by integrating the innovative and technological advances offered by online learning with the interaction and participation offered in the best of traditional learning". The integration of e-learning environment and traditional learning environment may combine ideally the useful aspects of both methods. E-learning environments ensure the flexibility and efficacy which cannot be found in a classroom environment whereas face-to-face learning environment provides the social interaction which is required for learning.

Need for the Study

Studies showed that blended learning was felt to have enhanced learning opportunities. Studies proved that the blended approach is a positive innovation to the learning experience. Blended learning environment has a favorable impact on student learning outcomes, is highly appreciated by the students. The utilization of email and class websites allows for interactive collaboration between students, teachers, and parents. Furthermore, it provides a basis for different teaching and learning styles that are offered by increased technology usage. Teachers' attitudes, will determine successful technology integration in an educational setting. Here comes the question whether the prospective teachers have positive attitude towards Blended learning, because the future generation; the future of the nation lies in the hands of the young teachers and the need arises for this study.

Statement of the Problem

Attitude of Prospective Teachers Towards Blended Learning

Objectives of the study

The investigator conducted the present study with the following objectives:

1. To find out the level of Attitude of prospective Teachers towards Blended Learning.
2. To find out the significant difference in the level of Attitude of prospective Teachers towards Blended Learning based on
    - Age
    - Subject(Arts/ Science)
    - Degree
    - Computer Knowledge
    - Internet Usage
    - Online Courses Studied
    - Locality
    - Residence

Hypotheses of the study

1. The level of Attitude of perspective Teachers towards Blended Learning is not satisfactory.
2. There is no significant difference in the level of Attitude of perspective Teachers towards

    Blended Learning in terms of the following attributive variables:
    - Age
    - Subject(Arts/ Science)
    - Degree
    - Computer Knowledge
    - Internet Usage
    - Studied Online Courses
    - Locality
    - Residence

Sample

In the present study, samples of 150 Student are drawn adopting the random sampling technique during the academic year 2013-2014.

Tools of Research

Self-constructed Questionnaire was developed by the investigator. Attitude Towards Blended Learning inventory consisted of 30 items, of which 23 items are positive statements and 7 items are of negative statements to be rated on 3 point scale.

Scoring

The maximum and minimum score of Attitude Towards Blended Learning inventory is 90 and 30 respectively.

Statistical Treatment

To analyse the data, the investigators used the following statistical measures.

Mean, standard deviation and't'-test.

Hypothesis Testing

Null Hypothesis 1:

The level of Attitude of prospective Teachers towards Blended learning is not satisfactory.

TABLE. 20.1: The level of Attitude of Prospective Teachers towards Blended learning

Sample	Number	Theoretical Mean	Obtained Mean
B.Ed Students	150	60	69

From the above table No. 20.1, it is inferred that the obtained mean value 71 is higher than that of the theoretical mean value 60, which is the frame of reference.

Hence the framed null hypothesis "The level of" Attitude of prospective Teachers towards Blended learning is not satisfactory is rejected. It is evident that the Prospective teachers have positive attitude towards Blended Learning.

Null Hypothesis 2

There is no significant difference in the Level of Attitude of prospective Teachers towards Blended Learning in terms of the following attributive variables:

TABLE. 20.2: Difference in the Attitude of Prospective Teachers towards Blended Learning

Variables	Categories	N	Mean	SD	t-Value	Level of Significance
Age	Blow 25 25 and Above	115 35	72.88 71.41	6.832 6.029	1.038	NS
Subject	Art Science	65 85	71.88 73.21	6.809 6.630	1.261	NS
Computer Knowledge	Yes No	114 36	72.78 70.89	6.764 6.071	0.900	NS
Degree	UG PG	112 38	72.80 71.80	6.850 5.899	0.690	NS
Internet Usage	Yes No	88 62	72.72 72.30	6.666 7.241	0.261	NS
Locality	Rural Urban	115 35	72.10 74.54	6.510 7.151	1.903	NS
Online Courses	Yes No	33 117	72.23 72.78	6.960 6.683	0.409	NS
Residence	Hostel Day scholar	85 65	71.95 73.60	6.530 6.903	1.493	NS

* Table "t" value = 1.96 at 0.5 Level of Significance.

From the above table No. 20.2, it is inferred that the obtained 't' values are lesser than that of the table 't' value 1.96 at 0.5 level of significance. This shows that there is no significant difference in the Level of Attitude of perspective Teachers towards Blended Learning.

Hence the framed null hypothesis "There is no significant difference in the Level of Attitude of perspective Teachers towards Blended Learning is accepted.

Interpretation

From the above findings it is inferred that,

1. Prospective Teachers below 25 years age have more positive attitude towards Blended Learning than the age group of above 25.
2. Prospective Teachers of Science group have more positive attitude towards Blended Learning than Arts group.
3. Prospective Teachers who have computer operating skills have more positive attitude towards Blended Learning than the group who do not have.
4. Under Graduate Prospective Teachers have more positive attitude towards Blended Learning than the Post Graduates.

5. Prospective Teachers using Internet for their studies have more positive attitude towards Blended Learning than the group who do not.
6. Prospective Teachers from urban area have more positive attitude towards Blended Learning than the group from rural area.
7. Prospective Teachers who did not study any online courses have slightly more positive attitude towards Blended Learning than those who studied online courses.
8. Day scholars have more positive attitude towards Blended Learning than the Hostelites.

Suggestions

1. Teachers should be trained in using Blended Learning both at School and College Levels.
2. Institutions must provide the internet access to the Staff and Students.
3. Students should be encouraged to use digital libraries at college and school levels.
4. As our country is a developing one, policy makers should keep the rural students in their mind and provide them Internet access free of cost.
5. Administrators should encourage and help the teachers to integrate technology in the classroom teaching.
6. Teachers should guide the students to use the technology in the right way and to evaluate the web resources.
7. Online courses should be included as part of the curriculum from the school level.
8. Submitting assignments through online, Computer made tests and assessments should be practised at school and college levels.
9. Flexibility to utilise internet for teaching and learning by the Teacher Educators and the students to support teaching, learning and evaluation.

Conclusion

The purpose of this study was to find out the attitude of prospective teachers towards blended learning. The adoption of innovations in approach to subject content and delivery will enhance the quality of students' learning experience and learning outcomes. Blended learning' is frequently not about learning but more about teaching. 'Blended teaching' and 'learning with blended pedagogies' better capture the true meaning of the concept. Providing Blended Learning teachers with technical and pedagogical support is very important for the success of Blended Learning courses.

❐

21

Effectiveness of Computer Based Multimedia Learning Material

Performance and behavioural outcome of the student is important aspects in school education here performance refers knowledge uplifted from the course of study. Behaviour outcome refers to social behaviour like responsible co-operation. Now a day complete is using in the entire field for the various purpose. In our education computer is used for giving instruction, administration and research. CAT, programmed instruction, PSI all is innovations in educational field to improve the performance. So the researcher has as her rightly chosen the study of the relevant effectiveness of computer based multimedia learning material on performance and behaviour outcome of high school students. The present study to find out the relevant effectiveness of computer based multimedia learning material on performance and behaviour outcome in Tindivanam Town. A samples of 100 respondents selected randomly were studied. A questionnaire method of survey was used to find out the effectiveness of computer based multimedia learning material on performance and behaviour outcome. The data were collected by using questionnaire as an instrument. Primary data were collected by conducting direct structured interview using questionnaire. All the respondents were asked the same questions in the same fashion and they were informed the purpose of study. T-test, One Way ANOVA and Correlation analysis was applied to test the hypotheses. The findings and observations are the result and outcome of the interpretations made during the study of analysis. The result found that there is a significant difference between traditional method and computer method of teaching.

Multimedia refers to any computer-mediated software or interactive application that integrates text, color, graphical images, animation, audio sound, and full motion video in a single application. Multimedia learning systems consist of animation and narration, which offer a potential venue for improving student understanding. Multimedia programme is an integral part of the educational technology. As a technique, it offers a high potential in application at different stages of education for the purpose of enhancing the teaching and learning processes, as is evident from the experience of developed countries.

The integration of multimedia technology into the communication environment has the potential to transform the students from passive recipients of information to active participants in a media-rich learning process. The introduction of multimedia or any other computer-based information technology is not intended to substitute a presenter. This new technology is intended to provide the presenter with a powerful tool that can greatly enhance communication by delivering a multisensory experience. With interactive multimedia technology, a teacher can communicate with the students by means of a presentation that becomes more than message-it becomes an active, exciting experience in a multisensory environment to create a multisensory experience. Multimedia reaches users in many different ways, enabling them to retain more knowledge and increase their understanding.

There are 4 steps in learning like attention, rehearsal, encoding and retrieval. A well designed multimedia application demands the simultaneous attention of several senses through dual encoding or the process of appealing to more than one sense simultaneously. Dual encoding facilitates and enhances the rehearsal process. Multimedia helps retrieval by associating sound, text and images with the concept being presented. Using text, images, animation and sound simultaneously greatly improves the students' retention of the knowledge and directs the students' attention to classroom (Louis, 2001).

Multimedia consists of the combination of video and movie clips and sound, text and graphic files all controlled by a piece of software and a computer which is equipped with a sound card, a video card, a CD-ROM drive and speakers or headphone. Sometimes, there is also a videodisk player, which is controlled by the software.

Computer based multimedia delivers information in a variety of ways but achieves its greatest effectiveness through interaction. In the first case, music and informative knowledge combine to convey the message. In the second case, technology provides a more effective presentation wherein information, images and sounds are technically and aesthetically integrated, focusing on a single specific purpose. The ability of students to work independently and to receive instruction suited to their needs and learning styles is inherently attractive.

Review of Literature

Dalacosta et al. (2009) developed and studied the effectiveness of Multimedia **application with animated cartoons in teaching science in elementary education.** The results of the study provide evidence that the use of animated cartoons significantly increases the young students' knowledge and understanding of specific science concepts, which are normally difficult to comprehend and often cause misconceptions to them.

Jian Hu et al. (2009) investigated the effects of introducing a software program, named the Dental 3D Multimedia System (D3DM), into the education of a group of junior dental students in their preclinical practice. One group received their training program in the traditional way, unassisted by 3D technology. The second group received their training program in the traditional manner, but also used the D3DM to supplement their education. The results showed that the D3DM-assisted group achieved higher scores and also indicated that the usage of 3D multimedia PC software had a positive impact on several aspects of subjects' performance.

Kanmani and Radha (2009) studied the Effectiveness of CAI package in basic electronics teaching. There was a significant difference between the control and the experimental group students in attainment of knowledge level, understanding level, and application level objective in the gain scores. Hence, the experimental group students were better than the control group students in attainment of knowledge level, understanding level, and application level objective in the gain scores. It was inferred from the finding that the experimental treatment is effective to the students.

Korakakis et al. (2009) made a study on the **"3D visualization types in multimedia applications for science learning for 8th grade students in Greece".** The aim of the study was to determine whether the use of specific types of visualization (3D illustration, 3D animation, and interactive 3D animation) combined with narration and text, contributes to the learning process in science courses. The results indicated that multimedia applications with interactive 3D animations as well as with 3D animations do in fact increase the interest of students and make the material more appealing to them.

She, Hsiao-Ching and Chen, Yi-Zen (2009) examined how middle school students constructed their understanding of the mitosis and meiosis processes at a molecular level through multimedia learning materials presented in different interaction and sensory modality modes. The dependent variables included subjects' pre-test, post-test, and retention-test scores, showing their understanding of mitosis and meiosis process at molecular level. The results of the study showed that the group which used multimedia learning material has a greater amount of visual attention and consistent with their long term retained learning than the group which did not use the same. This study adds empirical evidence of a direct correlation between the length of eye fixation behavior and the depth of learning. Moreover, it provides insight into the multimedia effect on students' cognitive process through the use of eye fixation behavior evidence.

Anboucarassy (2010) studied the effectiveness of Multimedia in Teaching Biological Science to IX Standard students. The results of the study revealed that experiment group performed better than the control group due to the exposure of multimedia based learning. Thus multimedia helps the students to sustain their interest and also their retention power compared to the traditional method of teaching. The constant use of multimedia will make students understand more and achieve more in their academic achievement. Hence it was concluded that the multimedia approach is considered to be one of the best techniques for biology teaching at IX standard level.

Ponraj and Sivakumar (2010) studied the effectiveness of Computer-Assisted Instruction in Teaching Zoology in Relation to Learners' Personality. The major findings of the study indicated that achievement scores of experimental group students were higher than the control group students after the treatment.

Yusuf, Mudasiru and Afolabi, Adedeji (2010) investigated the effects of computer assisted instruction (CAI) on secondary school students' performance in biology. The findings of the study showed that the performance of students exposed to CAI either individually or cooperatively were better than their counterparts exposed to the conventional classroom instruction. Based on the research findings recommendations were made on the need to develop relevant CAI packages for teaching biology in Nigerian secondary schools.

Objectives

1. To measure behaviour and performance of high school student.
2. To assess effectiveness in performance of high school student
3. To assess effective in behaviuoral outcome of the high school student.
4. To assess effectiveness in traditional and multimedia method of teaching.

5. To find out relevant effectiveness of computer based multimedia learning material on performance and behaviour outcome.

Hypothesis of the Study

1. High school students do not differ in their average level of relevant effectiveness of computer based on multimedia learning material on performance and behaviour outcome in traditional method and multimedia teaching of entire samples.
2. Respondents do not differ in their relevant effectiveness of computer based multimedia learning material on performance and behaviour outcome in pre test on the basis of groups.
3. Respondents do not differ in their relevant effectiveness of computer based multimedia learning material on performance and behaviour outcome in pre test on the basis of type of school.
4. Respondents do not differ in their relevant effectiveness of computer based multimedia learning material on performance and behaviour outcome in pre test on the basis of parent's education.
5. Respondents do not differ in their relevant effectiveness of computer based multimedia learning material on performance and behaviour outcome in pre test on the basis of parent's income.
6. Respondents do not differ in their relevant effectiveness of computer based multimedia learning material on performance and behaviour outcome in post test on the basis of type of school.
7. Respondents do not differ in their relevant effectiveness of computer based multimedia learning material on performance and behaviour outcome in post test on the basis of parent's education.
8. Respondents do not differ in their relevant effectiveness of computer based multimedia learning material on performance and behaviour outcome in post test on the basis of parent's income.

Methodology

The methodology adopted for the study is explained in detail. The sampling technique, size of the sample, variables of the study, description of the tool used and administration of tool are elaborated.

Sampling Technique

The random sampling techniques used in the present study. The survey should cover all the aspects of the subject selected of the study others are inferred from a study of a sample group carefully selected to be representative of the total population. At time, the survey describes a limited population which is the only group under consideration. It involves a clearly defined problem and defined objectives. It requires expert and imaginative planning. Careful analysis and interpretation of the data gathered and logical and skillful reporting of the findings. There are different findings such as social surveys, market surveys. The survey method is applied to the analysis of existing social conditions including educational conditions and to the analysis of public opinion. So in this present study, the investigator has used stratified disposition random sampling method.

Sample

Samples of 100 high school students selected randomly were studied in Tindivanam Town. Out of these high schools as many as 5 higher secondary schools have been chosen by appropriate method. All the available high school students studying in each of this selected high school were chosen as sample. Stratified disposition random sampling technique has been used in the selection of the sample.

Data Collection

Primary data, required for the present research work were collected by conducting direct interviews using questionnaire. All the respondents were given sufficient information about the study. These respondents were provided with the same questionnaires. They were also informed that they have to answer in the same fashion.

Tools used for the study

Development of effectiveness of multimedia programme and Scale by the investigator. The scale for measuring the high school student's effectiveness of multimedia towards science in the study. This scale has as many as 25 statements of which 3 point scale method.

Analysis and Interpretation

TABLE3 21.1: Showing the Mean, Standard Deviation of Relevant Effectiveness of Computer based Multimedia learning Material on Performance and behaviour Outcome in pre and PostTest of Entire Samples

Groups	N	Mean	SD	r value
Pre test	100	14.79	2.69	0.346**
Post test	100	19.30	2.86	

Hypothesis

High school students do not differ in their average level of relevant effectiveness of computer based on multimedia learning material on performance and behaviour outcome in traditional method and multimedia teaching of entire samples.

The mean and standard deviation of relevant effectiveness of computer based multimedia learning material on performance and behaviour outcome scores of entire samples are 14.79 and 2.69 in pre test and 19.30 and 2.86 in post test. The mean score of all categories are lay in between ($M \pm 1\sigma$) value. So it is concluded that average level of relevant effectiveness of computer based multimedia learning material on performance and behaviour outcome of entire samples.

TABLE. 21.2: Showing the Mean, Standard Deviation and t-Test for Relevant Effectiveness of Computer based Multimedia learning Material on Performance and Behaviour outcome on the basis of Groups

Groups	Sample size	Mean	Standard Deviation	t-value	Level of Significance
Pre test	100	14.79	2.69	12.86	0.01 (Significant)
Post test	100	19.30	2.86		

Hypothesis

Respondents do not differ in their relevant effectiveness of computer based multimedia learning material on performance and behaviour outcome in pre test on the basis of groups.

The calculated t-value (12.86), which is significant at 0.01 level, confirms that there is a significant difference between relevant effectiveness of computer based multimedia learning material on performance and behaviour outcome on the basis of groups. So the null hypothesis is rejected and alternate hypothesis is accepted. Therefore it is concluded that pre test and post test groups differ in their effectiveness of computer based multimedia learning material on performance and behaviour outcome.

TABLE. 21.3: Showing Mean, Standard Deviation and T-Value for Traditional Method among the High School Student on the Basis of Type of School

Sl. No	Type of school	Sample size	Mean	Standard Deviation	t-value	Level of Significance
1	Government	75	14.73	2.71	0.37	0.716 (Not Significant)
2	Aided	25	14.96	2.67		

Hypothesis

Respondents do not differ in their relevant effectiveness of computer based multimedia learning material on performance and behaviour outcome in pre test on the basis of type of school.

The calculated t-value (0.37), which is not significant, confirms that there is a no significant difference between relevant effectiveness of computer based multimedia learning material on performance and behaviour outcome in pre test on the basis of type of school. So the null hypothesis is accepted and alternate hypothesis is rejected. Therefore it is concluded that government and aided school groups do not differ in their pre test score.

TABLE. 21.4: Showing mean, Standard Deviation and T-Value for Traditional Method among the High School Student on the basis of Parents Education

Sl. No	Parents education	Sample size	Mean	Standard Deviation	F-value	Level of Significance
1	School	86	14.82	2.75	0.58	0.560 (Not Significant)
2	Under graduate	8	14.13	2.03		
3	Post graduate	6	14.21	2.44		
	Total	**100**	**14.79**	**2.69**		

Hypothesis

Respondents do not differ in their relevant effectiveness of computer based multimedia learning material on performance and behaviour outcome in pre test on the basis of parents education.

The calculated F-value (0.58), which is not significant, confirms that there is a no significant difference between relevant effectiveness of computer based multimedia learning material on performance and behaviour outcome in pre test on the basis of parents education. So the null hypothesis is accepted and alternate hypothesis is rejected. Therefore it is concluded that different parents education students groups do not differ in their pre test score.

TABLE. 21.5: Showing mean, Standard Deviation and T-Value for Traditional Method among the High School Student on the basis of Parents income

Sl. No	Parents income	Sample size	Mean	Standard Deviation	F-value	Level of Significance
1	Below Rs.50,000	70	14.51	2.53	1.56	0.215 (Not Significant)
2	Rs.50,000 – 2,00,000	24	15.50	3.09		
3	Above Rs.2,00,000	6	16.00	2.65		
	Total	**100**	**14.79**	**2.69**		

Hypothesis

Respondents do not differ in their relevant effectiveness of computer based multimedia learning material on performance and behaviour outcome in pre test on the basis of parents income.

The calculated F-value (1.56), which is not significant, confirms that there is a no significant difference between relevant effectiveness of computer based multimedia learning material on performance and behaviour outcome in pre test on the basis of parents income. So the null hypothesis is accepted and alternate hypothesis is rejected. Therefore it is concluded that different parents income students groups do not differ in their pre test score.

TABLE. 21.6: Showing mean, Standard Deviation and T-Value for Multimedia Method among the High School Student on the basis of type of School

Sl. No	Type of school	Sample size	Mean	Standard Deviation	t-value	Level of Significance
1	Government	75	18.75	2.91	4.33	0.01 (Significant)
2	Aided	25	20.96	1.93		

Hypothesis

Respondents do not differ in their relevant effectiveness of computer based multimedia learning material on performance and behaviour outcome in post test on the basis of type of school.

The calculated t-value (4.33), which is significant at 0.01 level, confirms that there is a significant difference between relevant effectiveness of computer based multimedia learning material on performance and behaviour outcome in post test on the basis of type of school. So the null hypothesis is rejected and alternate hypothesis is accepted. Therefore it is concluded that aided school students (20.96) scored higher mean value than government school students (18.75).

TABLE. 21.7: Showing mean, Standard Deviation and T-Value for Multimedia Method among the High School Student on the basis of Parents Education

Sl. No	Parents education	Sample size	Mean	Standard Deviation	F-value	Level of Significance
1	School	86	19.34	2.87	3.19	0.01 (Significant)
2	Under graduate	8	16.75	3.01		
3	Post graduate	6	20.12	2.63		
	Total	**100**	**19.30**	**2.86**		

Hypothesis

Respondents do not differ in their relevant effectiveness of computer based multimedia learning material on performance and behaviour outcome in post test on the basis of parents education.

The calculated F-value (3.19), which is significant at 0.01 level, confirms that there is a significant difference between relevant effectiveness of computer based multimedia learning material on performance and behaviour outcome in post test on the basis of parents education. So the null hypothesis is rejected and alternate hypothesis is accepted. Therefore it is concluded that different parents education students groups differ in their post test score.

TABLE. 21.8: Showing mean, Standard Deviation and T-Value for Multimedia Method among the High School Student on the basis of Parents Income

Sl. No	Parents income	Sample size	Mean	Standard Deviation	F-value	Level of Significance
1	Below Rs.50,000	70	19.11	2.64	3.29	0.01 (Significant)
2	Rs.50,000 – 2,00,000	24	20.04	3.24		
3	Above Rs.2,00,000	6	16.00	4.58		
	Total	**100**	**19.30**	**2.86**		

Hypothesis

Respondents do not differ in their relevant effectiveness of computer based multimedia learning material on performance and behaviour outcome in post test on the basis of parents income.

The calculated F-value (3.29), which is significant at 0.01 level, confirms that there is a significant difference between relevant effectiveness of computer based multimedia learning material on performance and behaviour outcome in post test on the basis of parents income. So the null hypothesis is rejected and alternate hypothesis is accepted. Therefore it is concluded that different parents income students groups differ in their post test score.

Findings

1. High school students differ in their average level of relevant effectiveness of computer based on multimedia learning material on performance and behaviour outcome in traditional method and multimedia teaching of entire samples.
2. Respondents differ in their relevant effectiveness of computer based multimedia learning material on performance and behaviour outcome in pre test on the basis of groups.
3. Respondents do not differ in their relevant effectiveness of computer based multimedia learning material on performance and behaviour outcome in pre test on the basis of type of school.
4. Respondents do not differ in their relevant effectiveness of computer based multimedia learning material on performance and behaviour outcome in pre test on the basis of parents education.
5. Respondents do not differ in their relevant effectiveness of computer based multimedia learning material on performance and behaviour outcome in pre test on the basis of parents income.
6. Respondents differ in their relevant effectiveness of computer based multimedia learning material on performance and behaviour outcome in post test on the basis of type of school.

7. Respondents differ in their relevant effectiveness of computer based multimedia learning material on performance and behaviour outcome in post test on the basis of parents education.
8. Respondents differ in their relevant effectiveness of computer based multimedia learning material on performance and behaviour outcome in post test on the basis of parents income.

Conclusion

In the present study, the researcher arrive the following conclusion based on the findings. In the present study, science students have relevant effectiveness of computer based multimedia learning material on performance and behaviour outcome of high school students in Tindivanam Town when compared with other students. The researcher framed objectives and hypotheses on the basis of the above context. 100 samples were selected randomly. A standard questionnaire was used to collect the relevant data. After collecting the data they were analyzed using statistical tools such as t-test and ANOVA in the both groups (pre and post test). The result concluded that the all the science students of average level of relevant effectiveness of computer based multimedia learning material on performance and behaviour outcome.

❒

22

Usage of Internet for Education Purpose among Arts and Science College

Education plays an important role in building a creative society. Due to the revolutionary changes in the field of telecommunications and Information Technology, educational institutions may be transformed from "teaching centers" to "centers of learning resources". Language is a tool for communication, and the system of language is learned for the purpose of communication (Clark, 1978).Internet is also a tool for effective communication among the several developments in Information and Communication Technology. The usage of Internet, social network, you tube; etc will stimulate the creativity among the users. Usage of internet for hi-tech innovative learning will develop the creativity of the students.

Need and Significance of the Study

Developing a creative society is the worldwide objective in education. Internet learning allows the learners to have more control over their own learning to think creatively, analytically, critically and to work collaboratively. The role of internet communication mediums have increased in social and academic interpersonal communications(Huang,2010).However, the internet usage among the students for learning is considerably less due to lack of Internet facilities and skills. The purpose of using Internet has an impact upon the innovative learning of the students.

Student teachers are enrolled only from Arts and Science colleges. As a Teacher educator, to promote the hi-tech knowledge of student teachers, we should evaluate and know about the technology skill of students from Arts and Science colleges, so that we can plan hi- tech oriented curriculum for our student teachers. Hence the investigator feels the need to study the usage of Internet by students' population from Arts and Science colleges. The 'usage' is referred to as practical use of Internet application in day to day educational activities by Arts and Science College students. Five major Internet communication modes (i.e.websites, e-mail, social network, YouTube and blogs) were considered in this study.

Objectives

1. To find out the level of Internet usage by the students of Arts and Science colleges.
2. To find out whether there is significant differences in the usage of Internet by the students of Arts and Science colleges in terms of the variables namely
    - Gender
    - Subject of study group
    - Location of college
    - Nature of the college
    - Annual income of Parents.

Hypotheses

1. The level of Internet usage among the students of Arts and Science colleges is high.
2. There is significant difference in the usage of Internet among the students of Arts and Science colleges in terms of
    - Gender
    - Subject of study group
    - Location of the college
    - Nature of the college
    - Annual income of Parents.

Sample

A sample of 160 Arts and Science college students belonging to five colleges in Madurai in Tamil Nadu was selected for the study. Samples were selected by proportionate stratified representative sample techniques. To achieve the objectives of the study survey method of the research was used.

Tool Used

The tool consisted of 30 statements under 5 dimensions anchored with 5-point rating scale [often, as and when needed some time, Rarely, Never] to indicate the level of acceptance of students. The minimum and maximum scores of the scale were 30 and 150 respectively. The tool was finalized with consultation of the teacher educators and research experts. Reliability and validity of the tool was established.

Data Collection Procedure

The purpose of the study was explained to the students and ample time was given to go through the tool and doubts were clarified while administrating the tool.

Statistical Techniques

Mean, Standard Deviation, and t-test.

Results

i) Mean

No of Samples	Theoretical Mean	Calculated Mean
160	90	92.59

ii) Mean Value under Dimension

S.No	Dimensions	Mean
1	Websites	23.41
2	e-mail	21.26
3	Social network	19.48
4	You tube	19.43
5	Blogs	9

iii) Level of Significance

S. No	Variables	Category	N	Mean	S D	't' Value	0.05 level of Significance
1	Gender	Male	80	92.96	11.92	2.054	**Significant.**
		Female	80	89.13	11.63		
2	Subject of study group	Computer science	80	91.45	10.62	1.973	**Significant**
		Other subjects	80	88.23	10.02		

3	Nature of the college	Aided	80	93.213	10.93	1.720	Not Significant
		Self Finance	80	90.362	11.02		
4	Location of the college	Urban	80	91.62	11.73	1.909	Not Significant
		Rural	80	88.11	1.52		
5	Annual income of Parents	Above 3 lakhs	75	93.97	90.14	1.984	Significant
		Below 3 lakhs	85	11.65	12.81		

Findings

1. The mean value of Internet usage among the students of Arts and Science College is high.
2. The results obtained from mean value of different dimensions show that the majority usage of internet is through Websites and least usage is through Blogs.
3. There is significant difference between male and female students of Arts and Science colleges in the usage of Internet for educational purposes. The result is in favour of male group.
4. There is significant difference between computer science and other subject group students of Arts and Science colleges in the usage of Internet for educational purpose. The result is in favour of computer science group students.
5. There is no significant difference between the students of Aided and Self finance Arts and Science colleges in the usage of Internet for educational purpose.
6. There is no significant difference between students of Rural and Urban Arts and Science colleges in the usage of Internet for educational purpose.
7. There is significant difference in the usage of Internet for educational purpose between the students of Arts and Science colleges whose parents' annual income is below and above Rs.3Lacks.The result is in favour of students whose Parents' annual income is above 3 lakhs.

Suggestions for Educational Implication

From this research findings here are some suggestions for improving the usage of Internet.

1. As Internet has become an integral part in today's education, well-equipped infrastructure such as computer lab with Internet facility is essential in every institution.
2. The Internet usage payment in colleges should be providing at concession rate for the students.

3. The syllabi should have some online based learning topics for students.
4. All teachers should communicate with their students by using Internet mode.
5. All major students other than computer science should learn ICT oriented courses in a compulsory manner.
6. Parents should give opportunity to their children, [particularly female] for using Internet for their studies.
7. To encourage on line communication, teacher should encourage the students to submit their assignments only through e-mail, blogs, etc
8. The university should organize the technology oriented enrichment programmes for all students and teachers.

Conclusion

Only hi-tech knowledge can promote the creative society nowadays. Tremendous changes in education can occur through advanced technologies used inside the classroom. Only the teacher can develop the digital knowledge among students in all levels. Therefore the investigator suggests that apart from class room teaching, teachers should involve themselves in creative techno instruction and encourage the students to develop their software knowledge. ❒

23

Blended Learning Opportunities in Higher Education

In the 21st century, Learning through Information and Communication Technologies (ICT) and influenced most of the fields and in education as well. Then, ICT have offered a learning climate environment for the development and use of various methods and tools, in an educational environment with the developments in technology, Blended learning has gained considerable popularity in Higher education in recent years. This form of approach which combines face-to-face teaching with some technological aids has been widely used in teaching and learning. Although there have been attempted to define the term blended learning, and to understand how to make blended learning work best, considerable further research and experimentation are needed. This paper offers a precise definition of blended learning, objectives of blended learning approach,categories and elements in blended learning approach and the benefits and difficulties of blended learning approach.

BLENDED LEARNING APPROACH: AN INTRODUCATION

Blended learning (BL) describes a learning environment that ether combines teaching methods, delivery modes, media formats or a mixture of all these. It also refers to the integrated learning activities such as a mixture of online and face-to-face learning. In other words, Blended learning is a mixture of e-learning and traditional types of learning. It is mentioned as the integrated combination of traditional learning with web-based online approaches, the combination of media and tools deployed in an e-learning environment and the combination of a number of pedagogical approaches. Among the benefits of blended learning reported by recent research were (i) provide students with more control over learning; (ii) To foster critical thinking; (iii) To excel online assessment system and computer tutorials.

OBJECTIVES OF BLENDED LEARNING APPROACH

Three are varieties of objectives for implementing a blended learning program, as follows.

1. Improved learning over either pure traditional classroom learning or pure e-learning
2. Increased convenience (time, place and so on)
3. The cost savings may result from perhaps reducing the number of instructors
4. The e-learning component of a blended learning program can help ease the classroom space needs by have in students learn more from outside the classrooms. The freed-up classroom space can potentially be used for other purposes.

ELEMENTS IN BLENDED LEARNING APPROACH

Blended learning includes a combination of computer-based and/or online and face-to-face elements, and a mix of formats, media and methods, so the most appropriate and effective approach can be used for each part of the learning experience.

Formats

1. To work face-to-face with students work independently in a self-paced way
2. The place could be something like a classroom, community centre room, conference hall, computer lab, etc.
3. The students may work some of the time in a computer lab
4. The students may join online learning communities and discussions
5. Learners attempt web-based tutorials or activities

Media

Students of the Higher Education may utilize CDs, videotapes, audio tapes, books, newspapers, television, radio, online chat, computers, web sites, and games.Some of these media (for example, newspaper or games) are available or usable online or as a physical resource.

Methods

- One can work one-on-one with students
- Student may setup group projects
- The students of the Higher education may put different groups together to work on similar topics or project

CATEGORIES OF BLENDED LEARNING APPROACHES

The categories of blended learning approaches are as follows.

Enabling Blends

Primarily focus on addressing issue of access and convenience – for example, blends that are intended to provide additional flexibility to the learners or blends that attempt to provide the same opportunities or learning experience but through a different modality.

Enhancing Blends

Allow incremental changes to the pedagogy but do not radically change the way teaching and learning occur. This can occur at both ends of the spectrum. For example, in a traditional face-to-face learning environment, additional resources and perhaps some supplementary materials may be included online.

Transforming Blends

Blends that allow a essential transformation of the pedagogy – for example, a change from a model where learners are just receivers of information to a model where learners actively construct knowledge through dynamic interactions. These types of blends enable intellectual activity that was not practically possible without the technology.

BENEFITS OF BLENDED LEARNING APPROACH IN CLASSROOM

The following are the benefits to blended learning approaches.

1. Students can participate at any time
2. Students can collaborate on their own time
3. It can provide reduction in costs, time, labour, stress, etc.
4. Course documents are available to learner 24 hours a day
5. Flexible classroom scheduling
6. Class goals can easily be met
7. Uniformed class for multi-section offerings
8. Effective use of class time
9. Enhanced computer literacy among students and instructors
10. Using the World Wide Web resources to support class activities
11. Supply students with additional learning materials if they need them

12. Increase the quality of communications between the instructor and learner
13. Using interactive programs that produce quick feedback and an advice for any remedial work

DIFFICULTIES TO BLENDED LEARNING APPROACH

Despite the advantages, there are some difficulties with blended learning. These can be reduce or overcome. To avoid these points might reduce the quality of teaching in this mode. These might include:

Bias

Some people have difficulty using or accepting teaching methods that are unfamiliar or unconventional. In the case of computer mediated learning, some people cannot use computers well or prefer to avoid using them. Blended learning can be adapted to suit not only the learners but also the teachers.

Faculty Difficulties

Faculty compensation and initial difficulties to cope up with the leaning requirement to teach in this mode. Not all instructors are as effective in teaching blended courses.

Lack of Means

One may not have enough time, money, equipment, etc. E-learning classes cannot function if instructors and students cannot operate the necessary hardware and software. Some schools may not have enough computer rooms for every teacher to use one, a school may not even have computers at all, or a teacher may not have the time or skills to create computer activities for lessons. Training is not done properly because of lack of time with use of technological tools.

Poor Mixes

Learning methods and tools need to be used well in conjunction with each other. Careful thought needs to go into making a good blend.

Computer difficulties: Students might have different computers with different bandwidth capabilities. Students using only speed computers than others.

Conclusion

A common feature in blended lessons is that students work in pairs or groups to complete a task. Education is not just information transfer but also skill development and social interaction. Students learn from each other as they help one another through the tasks and observe each other as work. Blended learning can provide reduction in costs, time, labour, stress, etc. Normally this is achieved by using computers. Materials kept on line are easier to access, distribute, and reproduce. Material can be accessed instantly from many locations at any time. This saves not only time, it also saves money that would be used for printing and distributing, and natural resources that would become paper waste. In addition it saves learners from losing, forgetting, or having to carry texts. Teachers can more easily share work with other teachers, and teachers can more easily modify and upgrade his material. A blended learning approach can make his teaching easier.

❐

24

Developing English Language Proficiency among Rural Areas

This paper deals with the effective methods which can be employed in teaching English to the rural students for their enhancement. Today conventional teaching methods are replaced with modern techniques which rely hugely upon media resources. Teaching English with these modern techniques facilitate to foster a positive attitude among the rural students to learn the language which would make possible for them to meet the upcoming challenges of the day in an innovativeway.

English is taught only as a second language in India and there is a great difyference between the city-bred children and the rural children in adapting to English language. The city-bred children are exposed to a lot of methods of learning English with ample facilities and special training in schools to improve their Listening, Speaking, Reading and Writing skills which are the basic skills for learning any language whereas rural students have only limited exposure to learn English.

Status of Rural and Urban Students

The city-bred children are exposed to a lot of modules and they have the privilege of learning English through different methods. Special training is available in the city schools to improve the students' Listening, Speaking, Reading and Writing skills which are the basic skills for learning any language whereas the rural students have only limited exposure to learn English.

The training provided in schools, is purely theoretical and bookish and English is taught only in the exam point of view. Hence, even after twelve years of learning English as a subject the students hesitate to communicate in English.

It is high time to motivate the students, right from their school by creating an awareness regarding the importance of English language. It is necessary that the teachers who teach English in rural areas should be committed and have an honest approach to equip the skills of the students.

The available resources should be completely tapped so as to provide an encouraging atmosphere for learning and practicing the language. This paper deals with the effective methods which can be employed in teaching English to the rural students for their enhancement.

Today, conventional teaching methods are replaced with modern techniques which rely hugely upon media resources and teaching English with the help of such modern techniques fosters a positive attitude among the rural students to learn the language which would enable them to meet the demands of the day in a creative way.

Problems Faced by the Rural Students

To begin with, the first and the foremost factor is the Socio-Cultural and financial background of the family. As most of the parents are illiterate, they are not able to guide their wards as educated parents do.

Hence, the students' performance lacks parental supervision and guidance which is very necessary for education. The illiterate parents are unable to realize the importance of education and also they do not understand the importance of communication skills which plays a vital role in their ward's career.

As there is an increase in the ratio of rural students preferring for professional courses, the above facts should be considered and those students should be trained to meet the need of the hour.

The following activities can be implemented to improve the listening skills.

1. Watching English movies on Television
2. Watching talk shows on Television
3. Listening to speeches of great statesmen & politicians
4. Watching headlines
5. Listening to recorded speeches, dialogues, interviews and discussions
6. Listening to news bulletins, chat shows, commentaries, weather reports
7. The problems of English language teaching
8. The problems is the demand for English medium and introduction of English as a medium in some schools in each block in Government

schools in many states. In most of the cases English as medium is introduced without ensuring the essential resources for quality teaching through English medium.

9. Research indicates that learning through mother tongue is ideal for harmonious language and cognitive development To explore, discuss and reflect on the issues and problems relating to the quality of English language teaching-learning in rural schools in terms of teacher inputs, materials and opportunities for learning English and conditions for English language learning in rural schools;

Developing communication skill

To explore, discuss and reflect onthe issues and problems relating to the quality of English language teaching-learning in rural schools in terms of teacher inputs, materials and opportunities for learning English and conditions for English language learning in rural schools .

One reason that many English learners have a low opinion of their skills is that they're comparing themselves to native English speakers or other learners who have reached fluency. If you observe that your English is not as good as other peoples', you start to bad about yourself – imperfect, inferior, etc.

The aim and scope of language teaching

New challenges

- Translation
- IT solutions
- Language learning strategies
- Language awareness
- Intercultural learning

New pedagogy

- Challenge to native speaker model
- Comparative language awareness
- Cognate language learning
- Reciprocal intercomprehension and languaging
- Intercultural awareness

Motivation

Motivation is a thing that can increase students' determination and interest in language learning. Working in non-native environment, but bearing in mind that our task is teaching a foreign language,

We see Some Important Goals of Motivation in:

1. Fulfilling university requirements
2. Improving one's education
3. Improving critical and creative thinking skills
4. Increasing job opportunities and salary potential
5. Increasing global understanding, etc. A teacher should put a strong focus on the student's motives to be able to accommodate them.
6. To motivate learners' attention should be drawn to the definition of motivation.

The Impact of language in Rural Area

The imposition of English on students belonging to humble background and financially weak background badly affects their performance at the college level. Most of the families of such learners belong to poor farmer, doing petty jobs and have no exposure of outside world, current affairs, educational policies and development of government, politics and world panorama.

Students from such families and background find it difficult to compete with such standards followed in schools and colleges. With little or no English within their rural setting, they are unable to complete their higher education thoroughly. Only few of them dedicated or having a proper guidance complete their higher education.

Conclusion

The main objective of this paper was to provide teachers and stakeholders with an overview of the challenges teachers may face while teaching in rural areas. Some of these encounters were isolation, cultural adaptation, and misconceptions rural families have about education, motivation, infrastructure, and violence. The authors argue that many urban teachers are not willing to take the challenge of facing schools in rural areas because of the previous issues. The text continued by mentioning some alternative ideas to implement in order to help teachers move smoothly into rural settings, inclusion in the syllabus of cultural particularities in rural areas,the proper introduction of teachers to the community, the participation of the community in the planning, local support and the access to learning resource centres. Finally, it indicates that teaching programs should introduce pre-service teachers to the rural context as part of the teaching experiences to avoid misconceptions about rural schooling. This paper ends by calling policy makers to acknowledge teachers working in rural areas.

❒

Bibliography

1. Alebaikan, R., and S. Troudi (2010). Blended learning in Saudi universities: Challenges and perspectives. ALT-J, Research in Learning Technology Vol.18,p.49-59
2. Arbaugh, J.B. (2008) Introduction: Blended learning: Research and practice. Academy of Management Learning & Education, Vol .7, p. 13–24.
3. Ausburn, L.J. (2004) 'Course design elements most valued by adult learners in blended online education environments: An American-perspective', Educational Media International, vol. 41, , p. 328-337
4. Berson M.J. (1996) Effectiveness of computer technology in the social studies: a review of the literature, Journal of Research on Computing in Education,Vol. 28,p. 486-500.
5. Boyle, T. (2003) Developing Models through Blended Learning Strategy. Language Learning and Technology, Vol.7,p.104-110.
6. Chodavarapu jalaja kumari, Digumarti Bhaskara Rao (2004) Methods of Teaching Educational Technology, New Delhi: Discovery Publishing House.
7. Cuban, L., H. Kirkpatrick, and C. Peck. (2001) High access and low use of technologies in high school classrooms: Explaining an apparent paradox. American Educational Research Journal, Vol.38, p. 13–34
8. Dan, C., Sivo, S and Brophy, J.(2003) Pattern of Learning in a Web Based Class Room, Language Learning and Technology, Vol. 7, p.119 – 140.
9. De Freitas, S. & Mayes, T. (2004) Review of E-learning Theories, Frameworks and Models, Unpublished project report, Essex University.

10. Elke Mader, Philipp Budka and Elisabeth Anderl (2008) Blended Learning Strategies for Methodology Education. Educause Review Vol.7, p. 86–99.
11. Farouq H. Aziz Al-Rahman (2013) quality of Blended Learning courses. ALT-J, Research in Learning Technology Vol.22, p. 45–52
12. Graham, Allen and Ure. (2003) The Key to Teach Through Blended Learning Strategy in Higher Education. Beston, Harward Business School Press.
13. Hannon, J. (2008) Doing staff development: Practices, dilemmas and technologies. Australasian Journal of Educational Technology, Vol. 24, p. 15–29.
14. Heinze, A., & Procter, C. (2006) Online communication and information, technology education. Journal of Information Technology Education,Vol. 5,p. 235-237
15. Julie Willems. (2011) Qualitative Research in Education. Sanfrancisco, Jossey Bass Publishers. Kumar.K.L (1997) Educational Technology, New Delhi: New Age International (p) Ltd., Publishers.
16. Lidia Bilbatua and Alfredo Herrero de Haro (2014) Teachers' attitudes towards Computer-Assisted Language Learning in Australia. Australasian Journal of Educational Technology Vol.24, p. 20–34.
17. Mohammad A. Alseweed (2014) effects of the traditional learning, blended learning and virtual classes learning on university students, International Journal of e-Learning, Vol.6,p.71–84.
18. Nichols, M.(2003) A theory for e-learning, Retrieved from: http://www ifets.inf/ journals/6_2/1.pdf.
19. Ooms, A., L. Burke, T. Linsey, and C. Heaton-Shrestha. (2008) Introducing e-developers to support a university's blended learning developments, ALT-J, Research in Learning Technology Vol.16,p. 111–22.
20. Philip Rotich (2013) Barriers to the uptake of web-based technology by university teachers, Journal of Distance Education Vol.66, p. 61–69.
21. Parthasarathy. M., Ananthasayanam. R and Ravi. R (2013) Usage of Internet Applications among B.Ed Students, Indian Journal of Education, Vol.74, p.56-65.
22. Rama Chandra Dhir (2014) e-learning, attitude of graduating students, International Journal of e-Learning, Vol.12,p.51–64.
23. Shih, Ch. and Gamon, J. (2001) Web-Based Learning, Relationships .among Student Motivation, Attitude, Learning Styles and Achievement .Journal of Agricultural Education, Vol 42, p.45-53

24. Saminathan, G. (2014) Student attitude towards Audio-Visual Aids used by the teacher, Journal of Distance Education Vol.23, p. 33–41.
25. Thiyagu, K. (2013) B.Ed., Trainees perceptions towards Blended learning in teaching learning of mathematics, Indian Journal of Education, Vol.43, p. 13–21.
26. Vaughan, N. (2010) Perspectives on blended learning in higher education. International Journal of e-Learning, Vol.1, p.81–94.
27. Vilma Bijeikienė, Svetlana Rašinskienė, Lina Zutkienė. (2011) studies about languages. kalbų studijos, Vol. 18, p.78-86
28. Vijay Jaiswal. (2014) Perspectives on blended learning in higher education, International Journal of e-Learning, Vol.1,p. 81–94.
29. Wan, F. ,Shafie, A. and Janier, J. B. (2008) Students' perceptions towards Blended Learning in teaching and learning Mathematics, Application ,of integration, Technologies for E-Learning and Digital Entertainment. Vol 5093,p.162-170.
30. Wing AU, Dr., Greg C. R. Dr and Yates. (2013) A study of student's perceptions in blended learning environment based on different learning styles, Educational Technology & Society, Vol. 11, p. 183-193.
31. Yilmaz, M. B. and Orhan, F. (2010) Pre-service English Teachers in .Blended Learning Environment in Respect to their Learning Approaches The Turkish Online Journal of Educational Technology, vol.9, p. 157-164.
32. Agarwal. Binod Symes, Larry R. (Ed) 1994). Future of Computerization in Institutions of Higher Learning, New Delhi: Concept Publishing Company.
33. Alexiaq Leon & et al (1999) Fundamentals of Information Technology, UBS Publishers Ltd., New Delhi.
34. Best John. W. (1997). Research in Education. Fourth Edition, New Delhi: Prentice Hall of India (P) Ltd.
35. Dannis P. Curtain & et al., (1988) Information Technology, Tata Mc Graw Hill Edition, Tokyo.
36. Dignmatti Bhaskara Rao (2001). Information Technology. New Delhi: Discovery Publishing House.
37. Harrychand (1990) Techniques of Teaching, New Delhi: A shish Publication House.
38. Johnself (1985). Micro – computers in Education. Kent (UK): The harvester press.
39. Kothari. C.R. (1994). Research Methodology, Methods and Techniques. New Delhi: Willey Eastern Company.

40. Mandha, V.K (1998). Modern Techniques of Teaching Vol. I, New Delhi: Anmol Publications Pvt., Ltd.
41. Panch. Ramalingam (2006) Education and Information Technology, ASC, Pondicherry.
42. Paul F. Morrill, et al. (1986) Computers in Education, New Jersey Prentice Hall. Englewood Cliffs.
43. Sampath et al., (1984). Introduction to Educational Technology, New Delhi: Sterling Publishers Pvt. Ltd.
44. Suja (2004), Computer Awareness among Higher Secondary School Teachers o fTrichy. Unpublished M.Ed., Dissertation. Bharathidasan University, Tiruchirappalli.
45. Teresa, A. (1990) Effects of experimental learning style on Co-operative computer – aided instruction: Learning Disk Operating System. DAI: 52(5), 1991 1719-A.
46. Vanaja. M and Rajasekar (2006). Educational Technology and Computer Education, New Delhi; Neel Kamal Publications Pvt. Ltd.
47. Achuthan Sarala, et al (1993), Computer Technology for Higher Education, Vol.1, 2 & 3. New Delhi: Concept Publishing Company.
48. Aggarwal , S.M. (1997) Teaching of Modern Mathematics, Published by Dhanpat and Sons, New Delhi.
49. Aggarwal, Y.P(1990) Statistical Methods: concept Application and Computation, Sterling Publishers Pvt.,Ltd., New Delhi.
50. Annie James (2005) Teaching of Mathematics, Neel Kamal publications Pvt., Ltd., New Delhi.
51. Baker, A. J., Kessler-Sklar, S., Piotrkowski, C. S., & Parker, F. L. (1999). Kindergarten and firstgrade teachers' reported knowledge of parents' involvement in their children's education. *The Elementary School Journal,* 99(4), 367-383.
52. Best, J.W., (1983) Research in education, Fourth Edition, prentice Hall of India, New Delhi.
53. Chavkin, N. F. (2000). Family and community involvement policies: Teachers can lead the way. *The Clearing House,* 73(5), 287-290.
54. Christenson, S.L. (1995). Families and Schools: What is The Role of the School Psychologist? *School Psychology Quarterly,* 10 (2), 118 - 132.
55. Ferguson, George A., (1976) Statistical in psychology and Education, Fourth Edition Mc Graw- Hill Kogkusha Ltd., New Delhi.
56. Henderson, A. T., & Berla, N. (1994). *A new generation of evidence: The family is critical to student achievement.* Columbia, MD: National Committee for Citizens in Education.

57. John.W. Best and Kahn, V. James (1999) Research in Education, Prentice Hall of India Pvt., Ltd., New Delhi.
58. Kenneth J.Travers(1977) Mathematics Teaching, Harper and Row Publishers, New York.
60. Kirschenbaum, H. (2000, January). The principal's view. T*he High School Magazine*, 7(5), 26-29.
61. Kothari,C.R.(2000) Research Methodology,Wishwa Prakashan Pvt. Ltd.,New Delhi.
62. Kuppu Swami Aiyangar(1973) The Teaching of Mathematics in the New Education, Universal Publications.,New Delhi.
63. Langdon, C. A., & Vesper, N. (2000). The sixth Phi Delta Kappa poll of teachers' attitudes toward the public schools. *Phi Delta Kappan,* 81(8), 607-611.
64. Lokesh Koul,(1997) Methodology of Educational Research,Vikas Publishing House Pvt.,Ltd., New Delhi.
65. Nanda. N and Gill. P.S. (1976) Teaching of Mathematics,Sharda Brothers Educational Publishers, Ludhiana.
66. Pillai. R.S.N.,and Bagavathi,V.(2000)Statistics, Sultan chand and co Ltd.,New Delhi.
67. Rai, B.C (1985) Methods of teaching Mathematics, Prakashan Kendra. Lucknow.
68. Ramirez, A. Y. (1999). Survey on teachers' attitudes regarding parents and parental involvement. *School Community Journal,* 9 (2), 21-39.
69. Rose, L. C., Gallup, A. M., & Elam, S. M. (1997). The 29th Annual Phi Delta Kappa/Gallup Poll of the public's attitudes toward the public schools. *Phi Delta Kappan,* 79(1), 41-56.
70. Rumberger, R. W., Ghatak, R., Poulos, G., Ritter, P. L., & Dornbusch, S. M. (1990). Family influences on dropout behavior in one California high school. *Sociology of Education,* 63, 283-299.
71. Shores, E. F. (1998). A call to action: Family involvement as a critical component of teacher education programs. Tallahassee, FL: South Eastern Regional Vision for Education.
72. Trusty, J. (1996). Relationship of parental involvement in teens' career development to teens' attitudes, perceptions and behavior. *Journal of Research and Development in Education,* 30(1), 63-69.
73. White-Clark, R., & Decker, L. E. (1996). The *"hard to reach" parent: Old challenges, new insights.* Fairfax, VA: National Community Education Association.
74. Abrol, D. (1977). "Some Factors relating to underachievement in English of Secondary School Pupils", Unpublished Dissertation, Karntataka University.

75. Aruna N.S. (1981) "A Study of Factors Influencing the Achievement of Standard VII students Belonging to Scheduled Castes and Scheduled Tribes whose Medium of Instruction is Kannada". Mysore University.
76. Bayley N. and Oden M.H. (1955) The Maintenance of Intellectual Ability in Gifted Adults". Journal of Educational Research", 52: 119-120.
77. Bhattachariya and Chatterjee (1986). M. A Cross study of Some Differential Aptitudes of Secondary School Students". Unpublished Doctoral Thesis, Calicut University.
78. Buch, M.B., Fourth Survey of Research in Education, Baroda, Society / for Education Research and Development, vol. II, 1991.
79. Connolly et al, (1994). Peer self- concept of adolescence: Analysis of factor structure and association with peer experiences; Journal of research on adolescence; Vol.4 (3), 385-403.
80. Choudary V.S. and Shoba Vaidya (1995). "Effect of Mastery Learning Strategy on Achievement, Sex, and Scio- economic Status of Students: An International Study". Progress of Education, LXVI (7).
81. Clark (1927) "Family Background and College Success", School and Society, XXV, 237-238.
82. Chandra and Sunanda Chandra (1985) "A Comparative Study of the Adolescent Boys and Girls in Relation to Attitude towards School Adjustment and Scholastic Achievement" .The Indian Journal of Community Guidance Service, Vol. 2, No. 3, September.
83. Aggarwal, J.C, 1995, "Teacher and Education in a Developing Society", Vikas Publishing house Pvt. Ltd., New Delhi.
84. Amarsingh, (1985), "A Study of Correlates of Job Satisfaction among Different Professionals".
85. Arora, Kamala, 1976, "A study of Characteristic differences between Effective and Ineffective Teachers" S. Chand & Co. New Delhi.
86. Badici, did a study on "Teacher Efficacy and Emotional Intelligence of Primary School Teachers", Nov. 2007.
87. Lokanath Mishra is a Lectured in education, Gramodaya college and Research Institute, Amarpur kashi, Moradabad, was presented a study "Reactions of pupil Teaches of two-year B.Ed., course towards Teaching and Teacher Education", January – 2003.
88. Natarajan, R. "A study on Organisation climate and teachers morale", Journal of psychological Researchrs, 2001, Vol.45, N.1,p19-p23.
89. Pareek, Ramesh, 1996, "Role of Teaching Profession" rupa Offset printers, Jaipur.
90. Rao, Bhaskara, D. 2003, "Job satisfaction of School Teachers, Discovery publishing House, New Delhi.

91. Sayed, N.A. "The relationship between cognitive personality and Biographic variables and preference for Teachers Behaviour of Secondary Schools Students". Ph.D. Educ. Kar.U., 1987.
92. Z. Zayapragassarazan is a lecture, Department of education, Pope John Paul II college of Education. Pondicherry and S. Pughazhendi presents a study "Perception of B.Ed., student Teachers towards Teaching practice programme", Feb.2004.
93. Arnett, J.J. (1999): Adolescent storm and stress, Reconsidered. American Psychologist, pp. 317-326.
94. Bailkeri, K. N. (1983): Effect of self- Instructional Remedial Micro Teaching course on the Instructional Competency of in service secondary school mathematics teachers.
95. Balachandran, E. S. (1981): Teaching effectiveness and student evaluation of Teaching, Ph.D., Education, Madras University.
96. Bhalwankar, A. G. (1984): A study of Reliability and Validity of the process appraising scale of teacher effectiveness.
97. Coates, T. I. and Thoresen (1976 spring): Teacher anxiety, A review with recommendation, Review of educational research 49(2), pp.159-184.
98. Cooper, C. Marshal, J. (1976): Occupational sources of stress. A review of the literature relating to coronary heart disease and mental ill health Journal of occupational Psychology, pp.11-28.
99. Cox, T. Mackay, C. J. Cox, S. Watts, C. and Brockley (1978): Stress and wellbeing in schoolteachers psycho-physiological response to occupational stress. Paper presented to the Economic Society Conference, Nottingham University England.
100. Dac, R.C. Passi, B K. and Singh, A. (1982): Effectiveness of different strategies of integration of teaching skills in developing general teaching competency of student's teachers department of teacher education, NCERT.
101. Davis, H. (1964): Evaluation of current practices in evaluating teacher competency, in B. J. Biddle and J. Ellance (Eds). Contemporary research on teacher effectiveness, New York, Holt, Rinehart and Winston.
102. Dohrenwend, D. et. al (1981): Stress in the community a report to the president's commission on the accidents at three-mile land. Annual of the New York Academy of Sciences 365, 159-174.
103. Donald, M. Medley (1982): eacher Effectiveness" Encyclopedia of Educational Research, Education Harold. E. Mitzel, Vol. 4. Mac millan publishing &Co., New York.
104. Fimian, M. J. and Santoro, T.M. (1983): sources and manifestations of occupational stress and reported by full item special education teachers. Exceptional children, pp. 540-543.

105. Folkman, S. and Lazarus, R. S.(1985): If it changes it must be a prosess: Study of emotion and coping during three stages of a college examination. Journal of personality and social psychology, 48, 150-170.
106. Girdano, D.E. and Everly, G. S. (1979): Controlling stress and tension, Englewood cliffs, N.J. Prinetice hall.
107. Greenwood, G.E. Olejuik, S. F. and Parkoy, F. W. (1990): Relationship between four teacher efficiency belief patterns and selected teacher characteristics. Journal of research and development in education,23 (2), 102-106.
108. Gupta, N. and Beehr, T.A. (1973): "Job stress and employee behavior", Organization behaviors and human performance, pp. 373-387.
109. Gupta, S. (1981): A comparative study of Socio-Economic background problems and professional behavior of men women teachers in co-education Institutions at different levels in the state of Haryana, Ph.D., Education, Kurnool University.
110. Gupta, U. (1981): job involvement and need patterns of primary school teachers in relation to teaching effectiveness Ph.D. Education, All Universities.
111. Hodge, J. and Marker (1978): assuring teacher stress; Beneficial task for administrator, American secondary Education, 8(4).
112. Joseph schwrzwaldet at stress reaction of school age children to the Bombardment by send missiles journal of Abnormal Psychology 1993, Vol. 102, No.3, 404-410.
113. Kaiser, J.S. and Polezynski, J. J. (1982): Educational stress sources, reaction, preventions. Poe body journal of education 10.
114. Kessler, R. C. Price, R.H. and Wortman, C. B. (1985): social factors in phycho pathology, stress support and coping process, annual review of psychology 36, 531-572.
115. Kryiacane and Suteliffe, J. (1977): Teacher Stress; A review educational review 29.
116. Kryiacau, C. and Sutclifee, J. (1978): Teacher stress; Prevalence, Source nd Symptoms, British journal of educational psychology 48.
117. Lazarus, R. S. (1993): Coping theory and research: Past, present and future. Psychosomatic Medicine, pp.234-247.
118. Lazarus, S. Folkman (1984): Stress appraisal and coping, New York springer publishing company.
119. Lislie Sovoy (1990): "Source of stress on trainee lectures for further and higher education". Journal for Higher education summer (1990).
120. Vene, M.R. (1985): A study of some of the personality components of creative student teacher in relation to their competency towards teaching.

121. Yogendra Kumar and Rattan Lai (1980): Use of micro-teaching in improving general teaching competency of in service teachers.
122. Best,J.W, Research in Education, Prentice – Hall of India (P) Ltd., New Delhi.
123. Lokesh Koul.(2005). Methodology of Educational Research, Vikas Publishing House
124. (P) Ltd, New Delhi.
125. *www.ICTeducation.edu.au/.../Cocurricular_Surf_ICT.pdf*
126. *en.wikipedia.org/wiki/Virtual-Learning*
127. *timesofindia.indiatimes.com/city/.../Virtual-Learning/.../838583539.c..*
128. Felix.A & Jahitha Begum (2011) "An Awareness of E-resources related to ICT and Educaation among M.Ed Students and M.Phil Scholars" ICT in teaching and learning, APH Publishing Corporation, New Delhi, p.169
129. Nagarajan .K (2009) "Educational Innovations and Management" Ram Publishers, Chennai. Pp.135-185.
130. Natchimuthu.K (2012), "Need of E-Content Development in Education Today" APH Publication Corporation, New Delhi. P.76.
131. Rangarajan. P & Senthilnathan.S (2012) "Teacher Educators Attitude towards E Learning" Edutracks, Vol.No.12 No.1 pp. 21-32.
132. Boehm (2010), "Improving Software Productivity", Computer, 20, 9 (2010) 43-57.
134. Hemalatha Talesra &others (2013). Web-Based Learning, Authors press, New Delhi
135. J.Y. Bakos (2013), "Inter organizational Information Systems: Strategic Opportunities for Competition and Cooperation", MIT Sloan School of Management Ph.D. thesis, 2013.
136. J.Y. Bakos and M.E. Treacy (2012), "Information Technology and Corporate Strategy: A Research Perspective", MIS Quarterly, 10, 2 (2012)
137. Krishnamoorthy, R.C., (2012). Educational Technology Expanding Our Vision, Authors press, New Delhi.
138. Mujibul Hasan Siddiqui (2010). Technology in Higher Education, APH publishing corporation, New Delhi
139. Mishra, R.C., (2013). Teaching of Information Technology, APH publishing corporation, New Delhi.
140. P. Alpar and M. Kim (2013), "A Microeconomic Approach to the Measurement of Information Technology Value", Journal of Management Information Systems, 7, 2 (2013)55-69.

141. Ranjana Bhatia (2012). ICT Enabled Teacher Education...University News May 30 –June 05, 2012, pp7 – 13.
142. Learning and Teaching Scotland (2003) *Early Learning, Forward Thinking: The Policy Framework for ICT in Early Years.* Learning and Teaching Scotland, Dundee.
143. Anboucarassy, B. (2010). Effectiveness of Multimedia in Teaching Biological Science to IX Standard students. *EDUTRACKS, 9(5): 37-38.*
144. Dalacosta, K., Kamariotaki-Paparrigopoulou, M., Palyvos, J.A., & Spyrellis, N. (2009). Multimedia application with animated cartoons for teaching science in elementary education. *Computers & Education,* 52(4): 741-748. Retrieved March 20, 2010
145. Jian Hu, Hao Yu, Jun Shao, Zhiyong Li, Jiawei Wang & Yining Wang (2009). Effects of dental 3D multimedia system on the performance of junior dental students in preclinical practice: a report from China. *Advances in Health Sciences Education,* 14 (1): 123 – 133.
146. Kanmani, M., & Radha, M. (2009). "Effectiveness of CAI package in basic electronics teaching", *Journal of All India Association for Educational Research,* 21(1): 47-50.
147. Korakakis, G., Pavlatou, E.A., Palyvos, J. A., & Spyrellis N. (2009). 3D visualization types in multimedia applications for science learning: A case study for 8th grade students in Greece. *Computers & Education,* 52(2):390-401. Retrieved March 21, 2010
148. Ponraj, P., & Sivakumar, R. (2010). Computer-Assisted Instruction in Zoology in Relation to Learners' Personality. EDUTRACKS, 9(6): 34-37.
149. Yusuf, Mudasiru O., & Afolabi, Adedeji O. (2010). Effects of Computer AssistedIinstruction (CAI) on Secondary School students' performance in biology. *TOJET: The Turkish Online Journal of Educational Technology, 9 (1):* 62-69. Retrieved March 21, 2010
150. Larson, Lotta; Kuhn, Cyndi Danner; Collins, Royce Ann; Balthazor, Gerri; Ribble, Mike; Miller, Teresa Northern (2009) Technology Instruction: Fixing the Disconnect. Principal Leadership, v10 n4 p54-58.
151. Chen, Rong-Ji (2010) Investigating Models for Preserves Teachers' Use of Technology to Support Student-Centered Learning. Computers & Education, v55 n1 p32-42.
152. Eisenberg, Mike; Johnson, Doug; Berkowitz, Bob (2010) Information, Communications, and Technology (ICT) Skills Curriculum Based on the Big6 Skills Approach to Information Problem-Solving. Library Media Connection, v28 n6 p24-27.

153. Jun, Han; Zhuzhu, Wang(2010) Capability Building in Educational Technology for Teachers in China British Journal of Educational Technology, v41 n4 p607-611.

154. Lei, Jing (2010) Quantity versus Quality: A New Approach to Examine the Relationship between Technology Use and Student Outcomes. 2010.

155. Lesisko, Lee J.; Wright, Robert J.; O'Hern, Brenda (2010) Technology Integration: A Best Practice Perspective. Online Submission, Paper presented at the Annual Meeting of the Eastern Educational Research Association (Savannah, GA, Feb 10-13, 2010).

156. McGarr, Oliver (2010) Education for Sustainable Development in Technology Education in Irish Schools: A Curriculum Analysis. International Journal of Technology and Design Education, v20 n3 p317-332.

157. Ruzic-Dimitrijevic, Ljiljana; Dimitrijevic, Maja (2010) Challenges IT Instructors Face in the Self-Education Process. Journal of Information Technology Education, v9 pIIP-35-IIP-48.

158. Savage, Robert S.; Erten, Ozlem; Abrami, Philip; Hipps, Geoffrey; Comaskey, Erin; van Lierop, Dea (2010) ABRACADABRA in the Hands of Teachers: The Effectiveness of a Web-Based Literacy Intervention in Grade 1 Language Arts Programs . Computers & Education, v55 n2 p911-922.

159. Waring, Scott M. (2010) The Impact of a Technology Coordinator's Belief System upon Using Technology to Create a Community's History. Computers in the Schools, v27 n2 p76-98.

160. Hammet Gandhi, H. & Varma, M. (2008). Elucidating Mathematical problem solving through metacognition. *Journal of Indian Education,* 30(3).

161. Kaholan & Vinod uppal, (2007) Womens attitude and achievement in relation to achievement motivation, *Journal of Education and Psychology,* Vol. xxxviii, No 3: 198-201.

162. Live, Carl (2008) Formative Assessment Pre- Test to Identify College students' Prior Knowledge, Misconceptions and Learning Difficulties in Biology. International Journals of Science and Mathematics Vol.4.

163. LongDon, Bernard (2013) Genetics - Are there inherent learning difficulties?

164. Lovelace, M. K. (2005). Meta-Analysis of Experimental Research Based on the Dunn and Dunn Model. *Journal of Educational Research,* 98(3), 176-183.

165. Malini, Sujatha (2006) The Attitude of special and Normal School Teachers towards children with Disabilities.

166. Mary Lou Koran, John J. Koran (2006) Individual and teacher/class effects in aptitude treatment studies, *American Educational Research Journal,* Vol.17, No.3: 291-302.
167. Mary Lou Koran, John J. Koran (2006) Individual and teacher/class effects in aptitude treatment studies, *American Educational Research Journal,* Vol.17, No.3: 291-302.
168. Robert B. Burns, (2012) The relation of aptitude to learning at different points in the time during instruction, *Journal of Educational Psychology,* Vol. 72, No.6: 705-789.
169. Anboucarassy, B. (2010). Effectiveness of Multimedia in Teaching Biological Science to IX Standard students. *EDUTRACKS, 9 (5): 37-38.*
170. Annaraja, P., & Jenitha Rani, J. R. (2003). Development of Visual Basic based CAI package in Commerce and its effectiveness on Achievement in Commerce. *Research and Reflections on Education.*
171. Balasubramanian, N., & Jayaraman (2001). Relative Effectiveness among Different Modes of Computer Based Instruction. *Experiments in Education,* 29 (2): 9-13.
172. Chang, Chun-Yen (2002). The impact of different forms of multimedia CAI on students' science achievement. *Innovations in Education and Teaching International, 39 (4): 280-88.* Retrieved March 20, 2010
173. Dalacosta, K., Kamariotaki-Paparrigopoulou, M., Palyvos, J.A., & Spyrellis, N. (2009). Multimedia application with animated cartoons for teaching science in elementary education. *Computers & Education, 52(4): 741-748.* Retrieved March 20, 2010
174. Dawson, M. E., Skinner, S., & Zeitlin, A. (2003). Rules of Engagement: Proceed with Caution when Integrating Multimedia learning Tools into Existing Course Formats. *Electronic Journal of Science Education, 7(4).* Retrieved March 21, 2010
175. Diseko, R. & Van Der Westhuizen, D. (2006). The Design and Development of a multimedia Tutorial for facilitation constructivist Learning among Nursing Science students: A Design experiment. *Proceedings of World Conference on Educational Multimedia, Hypermedia and Telecommunications 2006, pp. 493-499.* Retrieved March 20, 2010
176. Garnett, P., Hackling, M., & Oliver, R. (1997). An Interactive Multimedia Package Designed to Improve Beginning Students' Understanding of Chemical Equations. *UniServe Science News, Vol. 8, pp. 18-21.* Retrieved March 21, 2010
177. Jian Hu, Hao Yu, Jun Shao, Zhiyong Li, Jiawei Wang & Yining Wang (2009). Effects of dental 3D multimedia system on the performance of junior dental students in preclinical practice: a report from China.

Advances in Health Sciences Education, 14 (1): 123 – 133. Retrieved March 20, 2010

178. Junaidu, Sahalu (2008). Effectiveness of multimedia in learning & teaching data structures online. *Turkish Online Journal of Distance Education-TOJDE, 9 (4), Article 7.* Retrieved March 21, 2010
179. Kadhiravan, S., & Suresh, V. (2001). Effect of Computer-assisted Instruction on Self-regulated Learning. *Perspective in Education, 18 (3): 161-169.*
180. Kanmani, M., & Radha, M. (2009). "Effectiveness of CAI package in basic electronics teaching", *Journal of All India Association for Educational Research, 21(1): 47-50.*
181. Korakakis, G., Pavlatou, E.A., Palyvos, J. A., & Spyrellis N. (2009). 3D visualization types in multimedia applications for science learning: A case study for 8th grade students in Greece. *Computers & Education, 52(2): 390-401.* Retrieved March 21, 2010
182. Liao, Yuen-kuang & Chen, Yu-wen (2007). The Effect of Computer Simulation Instruction on Student Learning: A Meta-analysis of Studies in Taiwan. *Journal of Information Technology and Applications, 2(2): 69-79.* Retrieved March 21, 2010
183. O'Day, Danton H. (2007). The value of Animations in Biology Teaching: A Study of Long – Term Memory Retention. *Journal of CBE - Life Science Education, 6 (3): 217-223.* Retrieved March 20, 2010
184. O'Day, Danton H. (2007). The value of Animations in Biology Teaching: A Study of Long – Term Memory Retention. *Journal of CBE - Life Science Education, 6 (3): 217-223.* Retrieved March 20, 2010
185. Ozmen, Haluk (2008). The influence of Computer-Assisted Instruction on students' conceptual understanding of chemical Bonding and Attitude toward chemistry: A case for Turkey. *Computers and Education,* 51(1): 423-438. Retrieved March 21, 2010
186. Ponraj, P., & Nellaiyapen, N. O. (2008). CAI in teaching Zoology. *Research and Reflections on Education,* 6(2): 18-21.
189. Ponraj, P., & Sivakumar, R. (2010). Computer-Assisted Instruction in Zoology in Relation to Learners' Personality. EDUTRACKS, 9(6): 34-37.
190. Prinz, A., Bolz, M., & Findl, O. (2005). Advantage of three dimensional animated teaching over traditional surgical videos for teaching ophthalmic surgery: a randomised study. *British Journal of Ophthalmology, 89 (11): 1495-1499.* Retrieved March 21, 2010
191. Pryor, Caroline R., & Bitter, Gary G. (2008). Using multimedia to teach in-service teachers: Impacts on learning, application, and retention. *Computers in Human Behavior, 24 (6): 2668-2681.* Retrieved March 20, 2010

192. Rotbain, Y., Marbach-Ad, G., & Stavy, R. (2008). Using a computer animation to teach high school molecular biology. *Journal of Science Education and Technology, 17(1): 49 – 58.* Retrieved March 21, 2010
193. Segers, E., & Verhoeven, L. (2002). Multimedia support of early literacy learning. *Computers and Education, 39 (3): 207-221.* Retrieved March 20, 2010
194. She, Hsiao-Ching & Chen, Yi-Zen (2009). The impact of multimedia effect on science learning: Evidence from eye movements. *Computers & Education, 53(4): 1297-1307.* Retrieved March 20, 2010
195. Thilaka Suresh (2000). Instructional strategy change on the achievement in biotechnology and attitude towards science among higher secondary school students. *Journal of All India Association for Educational Research, 12* (3 & 7): 14-19.
196. Venkataraman, S. (2008). Relative effectiveness among selected modes of CAI in physics in relation to learner's personality. *Unpublished Doctoral Dissertation, Annamalai University.* Chidambaram.
197. Vernadakis, N., Zetou, E., Tsitskari, E., Giannousi, M., & Kioumourtzoglou, E. (2008). Student attitude and learning outcomes of multimedia computer-assisted versus traditional instruction in basketball. *Education and Information Technologies, 13(3): 167-183.*
198. Victor, Adeosun Olufemi (2008). Relative effects of three Multi-Media Instructional Packages on Nigerian student's achievement in Social Studies. *Pakistan Journal of Social Sciences, 5 (5): 415 – 420.* Retrieved March 20, 2010
199. Yusuf, Mudasiru O., & Afolabi, Adedeji O. (2010). Effects of Computer AssistedIinstruction (CAI) on Secondary School students' performance in biology. *TOJET: The Turkish Online Journal of Educational Technology, 9 (1): 62-69.* Retrieved March 21, 2010.
200. BEST,J.W, (2003). *Research in Education,* Prentice – Hall of India (P) Ltd., New Delhi.
201. LOKESH KOUL.(2005). *Methodology of Educational Research,* Vikas Publishing House (P) Ltd, New Delhi.
202. SINGH.Y.K,(2005). *Instructional Technology In Education,* P. P. H Publishing Corporation, New Delhi-110002.
203. SAREEN.N, (2005). *Information and Communication Technology,* Anmol Publication Pvt.Ltd, New Delhi-110002.
204. Hammet Gandhi, H. & Varma, M. (2008). Elucidating Mathematical problem solving through metacognition. Journal of Indian Education, 30 (3).

205. Kaholan & Vinod uppal, (2007) Womens attitude and achievement in relation to achievement motivation, *Journal of Education and Psychology*, Vol. xxxviii, No 3: 198-201.

206. Live, Carl (2008) Formative Assessment Pre- Test to Identify College students' Prior Knowledge, Misconceptions and Learning Difficulties in Biology. International Journals of Science and Mathematics Vol.4.

207. Lovelace, M. K. (2005). Meta-Analysis of Experimental Research Based on the Dunn and Dunn Model. *Journal of Educational Research*, 98 (3), 176-183.

208. Malini, Sujatha (2006) The Attitude of special and Normal School Teachers towards children with Disabilities.

209. Mary Lou Koran, John J. Koran (2006) Individual and teacher/class effects in aptitude treatment studies, *American Educational Research Journal*, Vol.17, No.3: 291-302.

210. Mary Lou Koran, John J. Koran (2006) Individual and teacher/class effects in aptitude treatment studies, *American Educational Research Journal*, Vol.17, No.3: 291-302.

211. Robert B. Burns, (2012) The relation of aptitude to learning at different points in the time during instruction, *Journal of Educational Psychology*, Vol. 72, No.6: 705-789.

212. Bhan, K.S., & Gupta, R. (2010). Study Habits and Academic Achievement among the Students belonging to Scheduled Caste and Non Scheduled Caste Group, *Journal of Applied research in Education*, 15(1), 1-9.

213. Ifshan Bashir, & Nadhia Hussain Mattoo,(2012). A Study on Study Habits and Academic Performance among Adolescents (14-19) years, *International Journal of Social Science Tomorrow, 1 (5)*. www.ijsst.com

214. Jagannath. K. Dange., & Girish, T. (2012). A Study on the Relation between Study Habits and Academic Achievement among Post-Graduation Students in Kuvempu University, *Indian journal of Experimentation and innovation in Education, 1(6). http://www.ijeie.in/index.php/articles/current-volume/vol-1--issue-6-nov-2012/104-*

215. Mohd. Ghani Awang., & Suriya Kumar Sinnadurai., (2011). A Study on the Development of Strategic Tools In Study Orientation Skills Towards Achieving Academic Excellence. ISSN 1798-4769 *Journal of Language Teaching and Research*, 2 (1), 60-67.

216. Mawthohiaisan & Deepak kumar. (2011). Study Habit of Post- Students in Relation to Gender, Faculty and Academic Achievement. *Learning Community-An International Journal of Educational and Social Development*, 2 (1), 55- 68.

217. Nuthana P., & Ganga Y., (2007). Gender analysis of academic achievement among high school students, Unpublished M.Ed. Thesis, Karnataka University Dharwad.
218. Omotere Tope., (2011).The effects of study habit on the academic Performance of students: a case study of some Secondary schools in Ogun state, *Published Online By: EgoBooster Books www.omotere.com*
219. Onwuegbuzie A.J, Slate J,R., & Schwartz R,A., (2001), The role of study skills in -level educational research courses. *Journal of Educational Research,* 94, 238-246.
220. Patel & Patel., B.V.,(1976). Study habits inventory. In: *Second Handbook of Psychology and Social Instruments,* Ed. Pestonjee, D.M., Concept Publishing Company, New Delhi.
221. Singh Y.G., (2011). Academic Achievement and Study Habits of Higher Secondary Students, *International Referred Research Journal,* 3(27).
222. Brown, R. (2003). Blending learning: Rich experiences from a rich picture. *Training and Development in Australia,* 30 (3), 14-17.
223. Finn, A., & Bucceri, M. (2004). *A case study approach to blended learning,* retrieved January 15, 2008 from
224. Garrison, D.R.& anuka, H. (2004). Blended learning: Uncovering its transformative potential in higher education. *The internet and higher education,* 7 (2), 95-105.
225. http://www.centra.com/download/whitepapers/CaseStudy_BlendedLearning.pdf.
226. Godambe, D., Picciano, A. G., Schroeder, R., & Schweber, C. (2004). Faculty Perspective. *Paper presented at the Sloan-C Workshop on Blended Learning.* Chicago, IL.
227. Gómez, J., & Igado, M. (2008). Blended Learning: The Key to Success in a Training Company. *International Journal of Instructional Technology and Distance Learning,* 5 (8). Retrieved on 3 July 2012 from http://www.itdl.org/Journal/Aug_08/index.htm
228. Singh, H. (2003) Building effective blended learning programs, *Educational Technology,* 43, 51-54.
229. Anboucarassy, B. (2010). Effectiveness of Multimedia in Teaching Biological Science to IX Standard students. *EDUTRACKS, 9 (5): 37-38.*
230. Annaraja, P., & Jenitha Rani, J. R. (2003). Development of Visual Basic based CAI package in Commerce and its effectiveness on Achievement in Commerce. *Research and Reflections on Education.*
231. Balasubramanian, N., & Jayaraman (2001). Relative Effectiveness among Different Modes of Computer Based Instruction. *Experiments in Education,* 29(2): 9-13.

232. Chang, Chun-Yen (2002). The impact of different forms of multimedia CAI on students' science achievement. *Innovations in Education and Teaching International,* 39 (4): 280-88. Retrieved March 20, 2010

233. Dalacosta, K., Kamariotaki-Paparrigopoulou, M., Palyvos, J.A., & Spyrellis, N. (2009). Multimedia application with animated cartoons for teaching science in elementary education. *Computers & Education, 52(4): 741-748.* Retrieved March 20, 2010

234. Dawson, M. E., Skinner, S., & Zeitlin, A. (2003). Rules of Engagement: Proceed with Caution when Integrating Multimedia learning Tools into Existing Course Formats. *Electronic Journal of Science Education,* 7 (4). Retrieved March 21, 2010

235. Diseko, R. & Van Der Westhuizen, D. (2006). The Design and Development of a multimedia Tutorial for facilitation constructivist Learning among Nursing Science students: A Design experiment. *Proceedings of World Conference on Educational Multimedia, Hypermedia and Telecommunications 2006, pp. 493-499.* Retrieved March 20, 2010

236. Garnett, P., Hackling, M., & Oliver, R. (1997). An Interactive Multimedia Package Designed to Improve Beginning Students' Understanding of Chemical Equations. *UniServe Science News, Vol. 8, pp. 18-21.* Retrieved March 21, 2010

237. Jian Hu, Hao Yu, Jun Shao, Zhiyong Li, Jiawei Wang & Yining Wang (2009). Effects of dental 3D multimedia system on the performance of junior dental students in preclinical practice: a report from China. *Advances in Health Sciences Education, 14(1): 123 - 133.* Retrieved March 20, 2010

238. Junaidu, Sahalu (2008). Effectiveness of multimedia in learning & teaching data structures online. *Turkish Online Journal of Distance Education-TOJDE, 9(4),* Article 7. Retrieved March 21, 2010

239. Kadhiravan, S., & Suresh, V. (2001). Effect of Computer-assisted Instruction on Self-regulated Learning. *Perspective in Education,* 18 (3): 161-169.

240. Kanmani, M., & Radha, M. (2009). "Effectiveness of CAI package in basic electronics teaching", *Journal of All India Association for Educational Research,* 21(1): 47-50.

242. Korakakis, G., Pavlatou, E.A., Palyvos, J. A., & Spyrellis N. (2009). 3D visualization types in multimedia applications for science learning: A case study for 8th grade students in Greece. *Computers & Education, 52(2): 390-401.* Retrieved March 21, 2010

243. Liao, Yuen-kuang & Chen, Yu-wen (2007). The Effect of Computer Simulation Instruction on Student Learning: A Meta-analysis of Studies in Taiwan. *Journal of Information Technology and Applications,* 2 (2): 69-79. Retrieved March 21, 2010

244. O'Day, Danton H. (2007). The value of Animations in Biology Teaching: A Study of Long – Term Memory Retention. *Journal of CBE - Life Science Education, 6 (3): 217-223.* Retrieved March 20, 2010

245. O'Day, Danton H. (2007). The value of Animations in Biology Teaching: A Study of Long – Term Memory Retention. *Journal of CBE - Life Science Education, 6 (3): 217-223.* Retrieved March 20, 2010

246. Ozmen, Haluk (2008). The influence of Computer-Assisted Instruction on students' conceptual understanding of chemical Bonding and Attitude toward chemistry: A case for Turkey. *Computers and Education,* 51(1): 423-438. Retrieved March 21, 2010

247. Ponraj, P., & Nellaiyapen, N. O. (2008). CAI in teaching Zoology. *Research and Reflections on Education,* 6 (2): 18-21.

248. Ponraj, P., & Sivakumar, R. (2010). Computer-Assisted Instruction in Zoology in Relation to Learners' Personality. *EDUTRACKS, 9(6): 34-37.*

249. Prinz, A., Bolz, M., & Findl, O. (2005). Advantage of three dimensional animated teaching over traditional surgical videos for teaching ophthalmic surgery: a randomised study. *British Journal of Ophthalmology,* 89 (11): 1495-1499. Retrieved March 21, 2010

250. Pryor, Caroline R., & Bitter, Gary G. (2008). Using multimedia to teach in-service teachers: Impacts on learning, application, and retention. *Computers in Human Behavior,* 24 (6): 2668-2681. Retrieved March 20, 2010

251. Rotbain, Y., Marbach-Ad, G., & Stavy, R. (2008). Using a computer animation to teach high school molecular biology. *Journal of Science Education and Technology,* 17(1): 49 – 58.

252. Segers, E., & Verhoeven, L. (2002). Multimedia support of early literacy learning. *Computers and Education,* 39 (3): 207-221. Retrieved March 20, 2010

253. She, Hsiao-Ching & Chen, Yi-Zen (2009). The impact of multimedia effect on science learning: Evidence from eye movements. *Computers & Education,* 53(4): 1297-1307. Retrieved March 20, 2010

254. Thilaka Suresh (2000). Instructional strategy change on the achievement in biotechnology and attitude towards science among higher secondary school students. *Journal of All India Association for Educational Research,* 12(3 & 7): 14-19.

255. Venkataraman, S. (2008). Relative effectiveness among selected modes of CAI in physics in relation to learner's personality. *Unpublished Doctoral Dissertation,* Annamalai University. Chidambaram.
256. Vernadakis, N., Zetou, E., Tsitskari, E., Giannousi, M., & Kioumourtzoglou, E. (2008). Student attitude and learning outcomes of multimedia computer-assisted versus traditional instruction in basketball. *Education and Information Technologies,* 13(3): 167-183.
257. Victor, Adeosun Olufemi (2008). Relative effects of three Multi-Media Instructional Packages on Nigerian student's achievement in Social Studies. *Pakistan Journal of Social Sciences, 5 (5): 415 – 420.* Retrieved March 20, 2010
258. Yusuf, Mudasiru O., & Afolabi, Adedeji O. (2010). Effects of Computer AssistedIinstruction (CAI) on Secondary School students' performance in biology. *TOJET: The Turkish Online Journal of Educational Technology, 9 (1): 62-69.* Retrieved March 21, 2010.
259. Jyotsna saxena, Manoj kumar saxena, Sandhya Gihar, ICT in Professional Education, A.P.H.Publishing corporation,2010, New DELHI.
260. Kamatchi, ICT For Social Change,Edutracks,Vol.11-No.12, Aug, 2012
261. Parthasarathy, Ananthasayanum, Ravi, Usage of Internet Applications among B.Ed students, Edutracks,Vol.12-No.7, March, 2013.
262. Anadakrishnan (2018).Higher Education of India. A Critical Viewpoint. University News, 56(41), 3- 5.
263. Bersin&Associates. (2003) Blended learning: What works? An industry study of the stragey, implementation, and impact of blended learning. Oakland, CA: Bersin& Associates.
264. Bonk, C.J., Olson, T., Wisher, R.A., & Orvis, K.L (2002). Learning from focus groups: An examination of blended learning. Journal of Distance Education, 17(3), 97-118.
265. Collis, B., Bruijstens, H., & van der veen, J.K (2003). Course redesign for blended learning: Modern optics for technical professionals. International Journal of Continuing Engineering Education and Lifelong Learning, 13 (1/2), 22-38.
266. Cottrell, D., & Robison, R. (2003). Blended learning in an accounting course. Quarterly Review of distance Education, 4(3), 261-269.
267. Driscoll, M. (2002, March 1). Blended: learning: Let's get beyond the hype. E-Leaning.
268. Graham, C.R., Allen, S., &Ure, D. (2003). Blended learning environments; A review of the research literature. Unpublished manuscript, Provo, UT.
269. Graham, C.R., Allen, S., &Ure, D. (2005). Benefits and challenges of blended learning environments. In M. Khosrow – pour (Ed.),

Encyclopedia of information science and technology (pp.253-259). Hershey, PA: Idea Group.

270. Martyn, M. (2003). The hybrid online model: Good practice. Educause Quarterly, 26 (1), 18-23.
271. Morgan, K.R (2002). Blended learning: A strategic action plan for a new campus. Seminole: Unversity of Central Florida.
272. Orey, M. (2002a). Definition of Blended learning. University of Georgia. Retrieved February 21, 2003, from Http:// www.arches.uga.edu/ ~ mikeorey/ blended learning.
273. Rooney, J.E. (2003). Blended learning opportunities to enhance educational programming and meetings. Association Management, 55 (5), 26-32.
274. Singh, H., &Reed,C. (2001). A white paper: Achieving success with blended learning. Centra software. Retrieved July 12,2005, from http:// www.centra.com / download/ whitepapers/ blended learning.pdf.
275. Ward,J., & Labranche, G. A. (2003). Blended learning: The convergence of e-learning and meetings. Franchising World, 35(4), 22-23.
276. West, R. e., & Graham, C.R.(2005). Five powerful ways technology can enhance teaching and learning in higher education. Educational Technology, 45(3), 20-27.
277. Young, J.R. (2002, March 22). "Hybird" teaching seeks top end the divide between traditional and online instruction. Chronicle of Higher Education, p.A33.
278. Nora, A., & Snyder, B.P. (2009). Technology and Higher Education: The impact of e-Learning.
279. Orhan, F.(2008). Redesigning a course for Blended Learning environment. Online submission, 9,54-66.
280. Wonacott, M.E. (2002). Blending Face-to-Face and Distance Learning Methods.
281. Avery, L. M., & Kassam, K. A. (2011). Phronesis: Children's local rural knowledge of science and engineering. Journal of Research in Rural Education,.
282. Betageri, G. (2013). Impact of English language teaching on the communication skills of rural students. International Journal on English Language and Literature .
283. 3.Moulton, J. (2001). Improving education in rural areas: Guidance for rural development specialists. For Charles Maguire: The World Bank
284. Aungwatanakun, S., "English Teaching Methodology", (2nd edn.), Bangkok: Chulalongkorn University Press, 1994.

285. Ur, P., “A Course in Language Teaching”, Cambridge: Cambridge University Press, 1998.

286. Hedge, T., “Teaching and Learning in the Language Classroom”, Oxford: Oxford University Press, 2008.

287. Harmer, J., “The Practice of English Language Teaching”, (6th ed.), New York: Longman Group, 1983.

❑❑❑